Lessons for Leaders

And for Those Who Aspire to Be

Lessons for Leaders

And for Those Who Aspire to Be

by Ron Barnes, Ed.D.

Lessons for Leaders And for Those Who Aspire to Be

ISBN 13: 978-0-9776198-0-1
ISBN 10: 0-9776198-0-X

Publisher Contact: The Printed Page
4802 E. Ray Rd. #23-249
Phoenix, AZ 85044
info@theprintedpage.com

Cover and Interior Design: The Printed Page, Phoenix, AZ

The publication of this book is supported by a grant from Allison-Williams Investment Bankers, Minneapolis, Minnesota. Proceeds from book sales will be used to support the Raoul Wallenberg living memorial, which is sponsored by the American Swedish Institute, and leadership development programs in Arizona.

Acknowledgments

I didn't write this book by myself. Many friends and leaders were with me all the way. It's impossible to acknowledge them all, but there are a few people who deserve to be recognized for their contributions to my life and, thus, to this book.

I must thank now-deceased Keedy Campbell, formerly President of Lowe and Campbell, a sporting goods company in Kansas City, Missouri. He took me under his wing back in 1944, provided counsel, and almost as important, tennis racquets and stringing, so I could pursue the sport of tennis. In the spring of 1948, he called Dr. Sharvy Umbeck, Dean of The College of William and Mary and tennis coach, to recommend me for admission. My thanks to Keedy and to Sharvy for giving me one of the great opportunities of my life.

At William and Mary, I had two great mentors and teachers who have become lifelong friends: Dr. Wayne Kernodle and Howard Smith. I literally don't know what I would have done—or been— without their support and guidance. I am so glad they are still around—as are their great loves, Ruth and Betty—so that I can publicly thank the four of them for the time, effort and confidence they invested in me. Wayne and Smitty are two of the finest servant leaders I have had the privilege of knowing.

There are a few other individuals whose friendship and support merit a respectful, sincere thank you: Bob Greenleaf for the many discussions about service and leadership we had during the summer of 1968 on the campus of Prescott College; a friend since the forties, Bill Wickersham, for teaching me lessons about being an active, life-long servant leader—he is one of the best; and the remarkable, caring leaders in my Prescott discussion group—Carl Brown, Marcia Gatti,

Mitchell Gelber, Jim Holt, Nichole Trushell—for the great conversations and laughter we have shared together through the years.

Finally, to Betsy, the most important person in my life. I thank you for your help with this book, and for sharing your life and love with me these last fifty-four years. Meeting you, and then winning your heart back on the W&M campus in the Fall of 1951, was the best thing that ever happened to me.

Dedication

This book is dedicated to the individuals who have graduated from the Prescott Area Leadership program and other Arizona leadership programs who are dedicated to serving as leaders; persons now enrolled in educational and training programs throughout the country who are learning to become effective leaders; and leaders who are actively engaged in transforming themselves into servant leaders. You have my admiration and respect.

We need you!

Preface

Throughout my adult life I have been a student of human behavior and of leadership.

I'm in my 75th year; it's now or never time! Either I share what knowledge and experience I've accumulated regarding these two related subjects or I simply sit quietly and let what I've learned fade away.

I've decided I'll feel better standing by this stuff than sitting on it.

So, what follows are the most important behavioral lessons I've learned that apply directly to leaders and to men and women who aspire to be leaders.

During my adult years I have been involved in training and teaching leaders, conducting seminars for them, giving speeches to them, consulting with them, and counseling them about personal issues they were experiencing with employees, colleagues or family. In between all those sessions I've worked hard to be as good a leader as I could be at local, state and national levels.

Working with hundreds of leaders around the country has provided me with perspectives that I believe will be instructive—even beneficial—to you. If I didn't hold this view, I wouldn't have the nerve to ask you to take some of your precious time to read what follows.

During the 1970s, when I was Director of Seminars in the Center for Applied Behavioral Sciences at The Menninger Foundation, a now defunct psychiatric facility in Topeka, Kansas, we held week-long seminars for top leaders in business, government, education and health care. One of the ideas we shared with them was a motto:

"You don't have to be sick to get better." The same approach applies to leaders: "You may be an effective leader, but you can get better."

And that message is applicable throughout your life span: "No matter how well you are doing in your life, you can do better." I am obviously not a fan of people—especially leaders—who are satisfied or content with their lives, as you will certainly learn if you read on. I believe all of us can improve ourselves.

This book provides insights, suggestions, thoughts, ideas, and recommendations on how you can live a better, fuller life and become a more effective leader.

In addition to brief essays ranging from Porcupines to Dreams to Pepsi Machines, you will find one-page thoughts scattered throughout the text and a half-dozen longer pieces that require a fuller exposition, such as Leaders and Change.

As you read, ask yourself these questions:

What characteristics should a leader—and aspiring leader—possess?

To what extent is self-understanding critical to a leader's success?

What are the most important qualities a leader needs to develop to be more effective?

What are your strengths as a leader? Your limitations?

Do you have it in you to become a servant leader?

Have fun!

Ron Barnes
Prescott, Arizona
October, 2005

Contents

An Abnormal Leader

One of my mentors, the late psychiatrist, Dr. Karl Menninger, once related this story. A couple was picnicking in a park. Perhaps a hundred yards away, a mother, father and two young children were sitting on the ground, also eating a leisurely lunch.

Suddenly, the father leaped up, began jumping wildly about and proceeded to rip off his clothes. He then ran, naked, into the nearby lake and thrashed about madly for several minutes. The couple thought him crazy. What would you think?

Well, actually what he did was perhaps what you would have done if you were sitting on a particular spot that fire ants had already staked out.

Once the couple discovered the reason behind his strange antics, they decided his behavior was quite normal.

Then there's the wonderful story comedian Mort Sahl used to tell about a bank robber who passed a note to a frightened teller behind the cage. The note read: "This is a stickup. Act normal!" Promptly the teller responded, "What's normal?"

Both stories focus on a fascinating notion, that of normality.

A related question is whether you want to be normal?

And do you want your children to be normal?

Most folks would reply in the affirmative to these two questions. Certainly when we look at a newborn baby, one of our first thoughts has to do with normality.

But, return to that first question. When we think about a person's mind or personality, is normal acceptable?

I don't think so. When it comes to mind and personality, we admire abnormality, even though the word tends to scare us. Yet, we know that anyone who achieves something special is, by definition, abnormal. Entertainers and sports figures aren't normal. Nor are those we call geniuses.

And what about leaders? Do we want normal people to be our leaders?

I don't believe we do. We want them to be more than "just one of us." We want them to be strong, resolute, responsible, caring, dedicated, loyal, creative and wise—just to name a few of the attributes we expect leaders to possess.

The point is that for most folks, "normal" is associated with average or mediocre.

While we love the normality of young children, we hope they can grow into the kind of abnormal people who will bring distinction to themselves, and even leave the world a little better than it was when they joined us.

That's what leaders are supposed to do, of course.

Being an abnormal leader means that the individual pursues certain variations on the human development theme.

Let's use the example of a tree. From roots a main trunk grows. Young trunks look pretty much the same. They look "normal," in other words. It's where and how the branches grow that lends abnormality to the tree.

Branches are the variations—and it's those variations that give the tree a distinct "personality."

It's the same with people and leaders.

Some people's variations enhance their personalities and are nurtured by them. Some variations are pursued actively. This book is about the variations that men and women need to develop if they are to become effective leaders and, perhaps, pursue the goal of becoming servant leaders. By and large, readers will discover that the suggestions made are also those that will help them become better human beings.

A primary thrust of these writings is that the better you are as a person, the better leader you will become.

The Porcupine and Relationships

Remember your first day of school?

If you were like me, you had been scrubbed harder and dressed neater than you'd be for the rest of your school years.

My hair was combed tightly, I wore my first pair of new shoes, new short pants, clutched a brand new pencil, and carried a Big Chief red tablet with my name printed right on the front cover. Mom told me there would be a lot of new challenges. I figured I was up for them.

What I soon learned was that maybe I wasn't as ready as I should have been for new relationships. I watched the kids mingling and shouting on the playground before the opening bell. Some in small groups, comfortable with friends, and a few others, standing alone, like me—watching.

Amid all the heavy learning and difficult subjects, all the spelling lessons to be mastered, multiplication tables to be memorized, and books to be read, there were relationships to be forged.

For me, during that first year, those were the most difficult part of the whole learning process.

It's like that when you're shy.

Each relationship, each friendship, is an act of faith. Reaching out to another person isn't easy. Rejection is always a fearful possibility.

Learning how to handle relationships during those early years largely determines how people will handle relationships for the rest of their lives. To a significant degree, one's "success" in life is related to this "fourth R."

We all learn that relationships can be fun—and they can be painful.

What we learn (whether we know it or not) is the lesson of the porcupine.

It was the philosopher Arthur Schopenhauer who taught us this lesson.

He told us that on cold nights, porcupines would huddle together to stay warm. Yet, when they got too close, their sharp spines hurt one another. So, they spread out again—and got cold.

After shuffling in and out for some time, they eventually found the right distance at which they could keep each other warm without painfully stabbing the other.

That's sort of the way relationships work.

Kids learn they have to find the right distance with other youngsters. Get too close to some, and they'll get hurt. Stay too far away from others, and they'll lose the warmth of their friendship.

And here comes the lesson for leaders.

Effective leaders must understand the bigger lesson about relationships. They have to recognize that although the porcupine lives defensively—out of necessity—they cannot. Leaders must grasp the reality that in order to lead they must live *affirmatively*. Unlike the porcupine, they see that they must initiate relationships and reach out to others.

Otherwise they will not become leaders.

Leaders must learn to take the first step; that every relationship is a risk, but risking is the only way to build a friendship and a trusting relationship.

Every leadership position involves a number—sometimes a multitude—of relationships.

Unfortunately, some people have been badly hurt by the sharp quills of intimacy and decide to live defensively—like porcupines. This is especially true when one risks loving another person. When an individual says to another, "I love you," he is also acknowledging that pain and suffering is possible. But he also is saying that in choosing to love, the person is worth the risk.

The same holds for people (like leaders) who *care* about others, although the degree of pain and suffering is less than in a loving relationship. But, caring about another can—and often does—end with the caring person being hurt.

This is a tough lesson to learn—and live with.

Leaders need not only to understand the possible pains of trusting and caring relationships, but then move on to live and lead knowing in their hearts that all relationships involve risk.

What a leader must conclude is that the relationship he has with followers is worth whatever risk may be involved.

Just one more reason to admire leaders—especially those who care!

Thoughts on Leadership

Leaders, be wary of scornful critics. They tend to view reality as personally threatening, oppositional and adversarial. Consequently, they invalidate their senses while putting negative twists on their perceptions. The result is a repudiation of the realities that the rest of us take for granted.

And be wary of fanatics. The more fanatical one becomes about an ideology, the more that person loses touch with himself and the realities around him. His perceptions become so narrow and confined that he relinquishes his ability to process information about self and the world about him in an unbiased, dispassionate manner.

A not uncommon sequence of bringing an idea to fruition is that one person originates an idea; a second translates it so a wide range of individuals can understand it; a third speaks about it in a manner that arouses the populace to action; and a fourth leads those who are prepared, to act. Each of the persons has a particular skill. Rarely does an individual possess two or more.

Frequently, a person who is easy to lead tends also to be a person who is easy to fool.

Some leaders have the gift of casting their followers into the light while others want their followers to remain in the shadows. It's a matter of ego, isn't it?

As you lead others, try to empower them with an ambition and ability that will impel them to surpass you as an effective leader. It's like the goal of a great teacher, which an effective leader surely is. A teacher can have no greater purpose than to send on students she has prepared and encouraged who feel motivated to exceed the teacher's limitations.

Just Say No to Comparisons

When I was young I used to compare myself with friends a lot. I don't do that anymore. I learned it didn't pay. Let me tell you why.

Way back in 1948 I entered college and quickly became friends with another freshman I had met at a tennis tournament the previous summer. His class schedule matched mine so we spent considerable time together. The first few weeks of college were great; we didn't miss a pep rally, football game, or tennis match.

Then came the first exam. Jimmy and I prepared for it as we had in high school by beginning to study the night before the test and continuing until 3:00 a.m. We took the exam the next morning and waited confidently for the results.

Two weeks later the results were handed back to the class of 450 students and I was overjoyed—not surprised, mind you—to see that my score was 92. Since my last name begins with a B, I was the first in my seating area to receive a paper, so I showed mine off to people nearby, mentioning casually that I had only cracked a book the one night.

I was basking in my intelligence until a girl in the row behind received her paper with a score of 282. It never occurred to me that a perfect score could be anything but 100. In this case it was 300 and mine was the second lowest in the class. Only Jimmy's was lower.

That's when I stopped comparing myself with friends. Jimmy didn't learn his lesson; he flunked out.

Leaders, heed this message!

It's okay to learn from other leaders; it's satisfying to adopt a few of their mannerisms; it's realistic to pay attention to how they relate to their followers; it's appropriate to emulate their conscientious approach to discharging leadership responsibilities; and it's certainly all right to acquire skills by, for instance, observing how they handle conflictual situations and angry individuals.

But you do yourself no favor by comparing yourself to them.

You can't, under any circumstances, become them. You are unique and have strengths and limitations no one else possesses. Your task is to build on those strengths, try to minimize and overcome limitations, and become the best leader you can be.

The only comparisons that matter occur when you compare who you are with who you want to become, where you are as a leader with where you want to be, and what you've accomplished with what you can and want to achieve.

So, give it your personal best.

But do keep in mind that the top score may be higher than 100.

Ah, The Concisers

One of the fateful facts of life is that there are folks out there who are complicators, excessive explainers, and "concisers." I love the latter individuals.

You see, here are a few of my favorite words: Yes—No—Fine—Good—Done—Okay.

My favorite phrases run along these lines: You've got it—No problem—I'll do it—Consider it done.

There are others in both categories, but you've got the idea.

I love short, concise responses. I lack the necessary patience for long-winded answers, unless, of course, the question requires a detailed response.

Related to this are the people who have to make everything complicated. Suggest they color the banner black and they'll ask "How black?"

And, wouldn't you know, too many of these folks are leaders.

I can just about pinpoint when I began having problems with these sorts of people. I was in the 5th grade. I asked my teacher how to work a math problem and, as a consequence, had to listen to a dissertation on the history of some obscure mathematical theory. My classmates and I went through the whole year determined never to ask another question.

It was probably a year or two later that I learned how much I disliked the excessive explainer's cousin, the complicator.

It was at one of our Saturday morning football games on the neighborhood vacant lot. I was quarterback, so it was my responsibility to call the plays. As I recall, the meeting in the huddle went something like this:

"OK, Tommy, you block Billy; Sam, you center the ball then block Donny; Bobby, you go long." With four "man" teams, that was the standard play. In fact, I don't think we used any others.

But I had failed to take into account Bobby Matthews.

"Do you want me to line up on the right or left before I go long? If I line up on the right, I might run into the two trees, but if I line up on the left I could run over the hill into the street. So, which do you want me to do?"

"Left, and stay out of the street?"

"Why? There's no cars on this street anyhow."

"Because, the street's out of bounds, that's why. Now, Let's go."

"Okay, I'll go down six yards, then cut right, then go long for ten yards, then look back over my shoulder. You can hit me with the ball then."

As I recall, I hit him in the butt!

All leaders need to take a hard look at their communication patterns. Are you as concise and explicit as possible when giving instructions? If you get into long-winded explanations, are you aware of doing so? Do you have a conscious goal of making instructions simple? Are you aware of body language and other nonverbal clues when you're talking to your group? What priority do you place on answering questions cogently and simply?

Part of your response to these kind of questions depends on the thoroughness of your preparation. Prepare well and conscientiously for meetings and you tend to reduce the length of your instructions and responses.

Then all you have to worry about are those participants who haven't read this little essay and taken to heart what's written here!

Thoughts on Leadership

A challenge for leaders is to make tomorrow seem possible and exciting to people trying to make sense of today while attempting to understand and assimilate what happened yesterday.

Leaders should be aware that it's not how smart they are, but rather how much good stuff they can borrow from others and use to accomplish their goals.

If a leader stops being a student of leadership, she likely will become less effective as a leader.

If leaders aren't clear about what they are trying to accomplish, they can count on their followers being confused.

Whatever leaders and their followers create will be imperfect, but that doesn't justify accepting what exists.

There is no such thing as a crash course in leadership; being an effective leader takes experience, knowledge, skills and, most of all, a commitment to becoming a servant-leader.

It's a Turtle World

William James, 19th century noted philosopher and prominent deep-thinker, was giving a lecture on the cosmos.

He seldom tackled more limiting topics.

After completing his talk, while receiving the usual compliments from listeners, up walked a little old lady. She waited patiently until his admirers departed, then in a frail but insistent voice spoke to him. "Mr. James, you've got it all wrong!"

"About what?" James inquired.

"About the world."

Taken back a bit, but more than a little amused, the great philosopher asked her to elaborate.

"The world ain't as you describe it. If you knew more, you'd understand that the world rests on the back of a huge turtle."

Now intrigued, James pursued the topic by asking, "And what does the turtle rest on?"

"Another huge turtle," replied the lady.

His patience intact, a serene smile on his countenance, he requested, "Please tell me what *that* turtle rests on."

With a twinkle in her eye, the little old lady said, "It's no use, Mr. James. It's turtles all the way."

Since hearing this story I've been unable to decide which of the two principals I would have most enjoyed meeting. Both would have given me clear definitions of their world views. Hers would, no doubt, have been more entertaining than his. Besides, I admire her spunk.

But in my more sober moments, as I investigate my own view of the world, the lady's simple "turtle world" provides only a chuckle.

The world I live in is complex—sometimes unfathomable.

But that little story does stimulate my thinking about how our particular views of the world shape attitudes and influence actions.

And these views take on considerable significance when held by leaders.

There are leadership scholars whose world-views are determinedly intellectual. Logic, reason, and objectivity describe their approach to the world. Emotional responses are disdained and rejected, usually with disgust.

There are "touchy-feely" leaders who make decisions about the world based on intuition and emotion. Their affective world-view has no room in it for the analytical and rational.

There are the fervent ideologue leaders who regard any type of compromise with opposing world views as either stupid, misinformed or treasonable.

There are bigoted leaders who cling to the belief that certain minorities are inferior and deserve to be treated as such. Their world-views haven't changed over the centuries, nor are they likely to.

Sometimes our world-views are distorted, sometimes they make sense, sometimes they are off the wall, and sometimes they get us into trouble.

But one thing I feel pretty sure of—they need constant examination, especially by those who lead others.

When my views on the world begin to solidify, I know it's time to back off, reevaluate, and think again about why I believe what I do.

I urge leaders to do the same.

Otherwise, you and I just might decide that the world really does rest on the back of that stupid turtle!

Thoughts on Leadership

If charisma indeed exists, it is in my opinion and experience—a temporary descriptor. It's human nature to ascribe to leaders (and celebrities) that special, inspired character strength called charisma until, that is, people get to know them. Then they are recognized as fallible human beings, just like the rest of us.

Expect reason to be true to itself, not to you, leaders, and you will have taken a major step toward wisdom.

If you are dominated by the tyranny of "shoulds, oughts, and rules" that restrict your freedom and that of others, then you are unlikely to be an effective leader. That unholy trio has a tendency to alter circumstances to your satisfaction and bend people to your will. Better that you center your behavior on certain moral principles that guide, but not compel you, or insist that others rigidly comply.

If you can lead without somehow communicating critical judgments about the people with whom you're interacting, you'll have taken a giant step toward being trusted as a leader.

A leader who seeks to be esteemed will never obtain enough to be satisfied.

Servant Leaders and Society

I love a good story.

And one of the best is Herman Hesse's *Journey to the East*, about a group of men on a mythical journey. The main character is Leo, the servant who does menial chores but also sustains the group through his spirit and songs.

He is an extraordinary person. During the journey, Leo suddenly disappears, plunging the group into such disarray that the journey is abandoned. They can't go on without him. The story's narrator, also a member of the group, after years of wandering, finds Leo and is taken into the Order that sponsored the journey.

He then discovers that Leo, whom he had known as a servant, is in fact the titular head of the Order, its guiding spirit, a great and noble leader.

This lovely and profound story was first shared with me back in 1968 by Bob Greenleaf. A few years later, he made this story the centerpiece of his superb book, *Servant Leadership*. Few books and few individuals have had as much impact upon me and upon my concept of leadership.

In our conversations and in his book, Bob developed the thesis that the truly great leader must be, and must be perceived as, servant first. This is a key to a leader's greatness, as it was with Leo, who of course, was the true leader of the group but saw himself primarily as its servant.

Bob and I talked about what we saw happening in our society. We were concerned about our elected officials, how they led (or didn't), what motivated them, and why people held so many of them in such disrespect.

Bob expressed the belief that the only leader who deserves our respect is the one whose primary motivation is to serve. Further, he believed that people would only respond favorably to individuals chosen as leaders because they first had proven themselves as trusted servants.

Clearly, the servant leader is servant first. He or she gains respect for service to others and, thus, becomes a leader. How different from people who identify themselves as leaders first and whose need for power or material possessions motivate their desire for office.

Leaders-first puts their own welfare as the top priority while servants-first make sure that other people's highest priority needs are being served. The test, according to Bob, is whether those being served "grow as persons...become healthier, wiser, freer, more autonomous, more likely themselves to be servants."

Servant leaders concern themselves with the least privileged in society. They ask themselves if the least privileged will benefit or, at least, not be further deprived by the action they take.

I've reflected on Bob's servant leader concept for years now, and am convinced there is no better way to evaluate our leaders. Using this standard, it's easy to judge the priorities and actions of our community, state, and national leaders. Regrettably, we have too few servant leaders in office. But, I believe they're out there—if we want to find them.

Then we need to join them in their journeys.

Servant Leaders and Unreason

Josh Billings once said: "It ain't that we're so ignorant, it's just that so much of what we know ain't so."

He could well have been talking about the political process surrounding elections in this nation.

Now, it's axiomatic that leaders will be involved in elections. It's less clear to me why servant leaders would entangle themselves at state and national levels. Why, you may ask? Because the further the political process is from the daily lives of citizens, the more distortion and propaganda exists in campaigns.

And servant leaders are not the kind of folks who tolerate, or want to be associated with, distortion and propaganda.

At local levels—at least in smaller communities—facts tend to prevail. Candidates need to stay pretty close to the truth or the public and local media will likely call them on their transgressions. Statewide candidates from rural areas have much the same limitations facing them.

But candidates in larger cities running for local, state, and national positions tend to engage in election practices that bend facts and spin truths.

And I have trouble believing that servant leaders will choose to be part of this kind of political process.

For instance, how could leaders who put public servanthood before self-interest hire "handlers" or spin doctors to alter information, twist facts, and create propaganda in order to make themselves "look good" while, in the process, insult the intelligence and reasoning ability of citizens?

I can't imagine a servant leader trying to "be all things to all people," following carefully prepared scripts, and telling people what they want to hear rather than what they need to hear.

I believe servant leaders are more honest than that!

So, does this mean servant leaders are likely to decline opportunities to run for higher elective offices? I hope not! But, when they do run for public office, I believe they will run clean, aboveboard campaigns that will eschew propaganda and distortion. We will know they are servant leaders by the honesty and quality of their campaigns.

There's another issue that bears on the candidacy of servant leaders; I think servant leaders have great respect for **reason**.

And reason has little to do with the election process.

The fateful fact is, candidates who resort to reason likely will discover they are increasingly talking to the wall.

This issue is important for leaders to ponder, so let's examine briefly why politicians might choose to avoid using reason.

First, reason is boring. The logic implicit in reason rarely excites the public. To provoke emotions, politicians appeal to passions, which play in a different ballpark. Excitement is the goal; reason is dull!

Second, most folks tend not to deal with reason regularly, so they don't understand it or follow it easily. The snapshots of information that television, newspapers and the internet feed us lack reasoned details supporting the viewpoint a candidate is promoting. Professional communicators know we want quick, down-and-dirty stuff; readers and viewers tend to ignore semi-long treatises. Why? See #1 above.

Third, while candidates use words to describe their ideas, they understand that impressions and images are what we take to the voting booth. Sure, we want to match our favorite self-interests with theirs, but their superficial—and often conflicting—positions on important issues provide us with few definitive clues about what they will do after the election. Remember the "read my lips—no new taxes" campaign promise?

Fourth, I suspect Samuel Butler specifically had politicians in mind when he said, "If you follow reason far enough, it always leads to conclusions that are contrary to reason."

Reason, as presidential candidates practice it, serves to rationalize weak arguments, to justify positions that are popular with a targeted segment of the population, or to appeal to the biases, dogmas and prejudices of a specific audience.

Finally, reason doesn't "sell." And the selling of a candidate is what elections are usually about. Rational arguments based on reason are not what the majority of the voters remember or what sways them. James Harvey Robinson put it this way: "Most of our so-called reasoning consists in finding arguments for going on believing what we already do."

We tend to gravitate to candidates who identify with our primary beliefs or most critical self-interests and stay with them regardless of the campaign rhetoric. We know they must somehow pander to the majority and play the game called Political Hypocrisy.

That's not a game servant leaders will play.

So, when we observe a candidate using reason in his arguments, responding rationally to questions, and interacting with the media and public precisely and consistently, it's likely we are observing a servant leader in action. While the statements of such a candidate may be boring and dull, the extra time and energy we devote to understanding them is likely to be worth it.

We just may have a servant leader standing before us.

Servant Leaders and Politics

For the past several years I've been wrestling with whether I could envision servant leaders in state or national elected or appointed positions. I decided that while we most assuredly need servant leaders in those posts, it is likely many will choose not to work in the national or state arena. The previous essay provides one set of "reasons."

But there are other negative factors that discourage servant leaders from accepting political offices: dealing with huge special interest lobbies, working with self-important individuals whose primary concern is getting reelected, interacting with morally and ethically challenged politicians. A major drawback is that party politics takes precedence over the common good. Doing what's best for the state or nation means, to most party leaders, doing what's best for their party.

In other words, the political system itself is not conducive to the kind of independent, critical thinking that servant leaders demonstrate. I have trouble seeing servant leaders putting party ahead of the common good.

In early June 2005, an old friend, Bill Jamieson, spoke to the Prescott Area Leadership graduating class. Bill had left Arizona back in the early 1990s, after serving as director of the departments of Economic Security and Administration and working in a private consulting business, to assume the presidency of the Institute for Servant Leadership, located in Asheville, North Carolina. When I asked about his insights regarding servant leaders and politics, he sent two books written by his predecessor, Bishop Bennett J. Sims, former Episcopal Bishop of the Diocese of Atlanta.

In *Servanthood: Leadership for the Third Millennium,* Bishop Sims makes two points that are particularly instructive. First, he concludes that, "All leadership is the exercise of power." But a servant leader doesn't use power in the conventional way the term is defined—not as dominance or subjugation or with the kind of control that compels compliance. Rather, Sims tells us, a servant leader uses power "to make a difference," and that's the second critical aspect of servant leadership. Sims contends that each of us possesses this kind of power and we have the ability to make a difference in the lives of others and in the world if we choose to exercise it.

Bishop Sims underlines his points with two quotations that merit inclusion here: Jesus said, "Whoever wishes to be great among you must be your servant, and whoever wishes to be first among you must be the slave of all."

Albert Schweitzer wrote this: "The only ones among you who will be truly happy are those who have sought and found how to serve."

The power that servant leaders demonstrate is the power that is given away; that works through others; that makes others powerful; that elevates others; that heals; that provokes people to gravitate to it; that gives credit to others; that is inclusive. It is power *with* people.

It is not the kind of power that is hoarded; that exalts self; that makes the possessor powerful; that strengthens one's own position; that enables one to dominate and subjugate; that is used to exclude others. It is not power *over* people.

Power for servant leaders is collaborative and elevates partnership. It's not competitive and dominating. A servant leader understands that power that compels compliance is a dangerous approach that, in this world, at this time, threatens our survival.

Listen to Sims' words: "Servant leaders know this pull toward collaboration intuitively. Collaborative systems are designed around such factors as *shared vision,* a keen sense of *belonging* and the *courage to tell the truth* in all relationships. The reason that such collaboration lifts the spirit of human work is that it appeals to the *best* of who we are rather than the *basest* of our motives, encouraging the offering of everyone's personal gifts for doing and improving the work. Such systems enlarge and enhance the lives of their members. The secret lies in setting and sustaining the high purpose of goals of service that go beyond private satisfactions. This is true in all systems: families, business enterprises, churches, and nations in their domestic and global security. Systems fail when their leaders' exploit their people and practice deceit. Systems succeed when their leaders cherish their people and speak the truth."

Servant leader power is not some adolescent concept of dominance or toughness. It's tender caring and inclusive sharing; it's grounded in love and resides in one's soul.

All of us need to be aware that servant leadership is an ideal. Like education, it's a journey, not a destination. Each of us is a flawed individual; none of us will become a perfect servant leader, just as it's unlikely any of us will achieve sainthood. But, being imperfect doesn't disqualify us from working toward the servant leader ideal. Owning up to our imperfections is the only road that leads toward perfection.

Politicians, like the rest of us, have flaws. A relevant question is, "Are they working to correct and overcome them in the spirit of servant leadership?" I don't rule out the possibility that politicians can be servant leaders; I truly (and desperately) hope we see servant leaders gracing our lives and nation.

They are needed!

Servant Leaders and Fools

A few weeks ago I was having lunch at a local restaurant. At the next table were three men, two of whom hardly said a word. They were being subjected to the semi-cerebral views of an educated fool. I assumed they reported to him. He was a department head at a college.

Not since my days as a college professor had I heard such pompous, pretentious drivel. This man was propounding the extent of his intelligence and complaining about the limitations placed on him by his inferiors who ran the college.

Later that same afternoon I ran into a friend who shared with me some of his concerns about the community. This is a man with little formal schooling but a wealth of experience and learning. He's one of the smartest persons I've ever met.

Two men—one with a fine academic background, no doubt, but a fool. The other, a person with no more than six or seven years of schooling, but a wise man.

Both are leaders.

One, because of the position he holds at a college. The other, not because of any official position he holds, but because he is widely respected within the community for his insight.

I spent the rest of the afternoon thinking about foolishness and wisdom—and leaders.

I'm inclined to believe that far too many leaders are fools. I have also met leaders who possess wisdom. I believe the world is overpopulated with the former, and underpopulated with the latter. It's easy to become a fool, tough to become wise.

A fool can do nothing and still qualify. Or, can attend school, gain degrees, accumulate knowledge, become wealthy, get elected to public office, and be hailed as a leader. The roads to "fooldom" are remarkably diverse.

Not so the road to wisdom.

I believe a leader who achieves a degree of wisdom must, above all else, seek to be a servant leader. In addition, it is necessary to develop a balanced perspective, uncommon sense, and the ability to learn from experience.

For me, a balanced perspective means an openness to new experiences, an insatiable curiosity, flexible attitudes and approaches to life, and a commitment to being as objective as possible in a subjective world. It's the cultivated ability to weigh choices, balance inconsistencies, compare differences, and identify nonsense.

Uncommon sense is a more precious and rare kind of smarts than schooled learning, high intelligence, or ordinary common sense. Schooling insures that people know certain things; intelligence tells us something about the mind, but nothing about the heart or spirit; common sense is nothing more than common—most of us possess some. But uncommon sense is the ability to look at the same world the rest of us do and see the connections, meanings, and messages others don't.

As for experience, we all have it, but relatively few of us are able to learn much from it. Life is rich in edifying opportunities that enable us to benefit from both successes and mistakes. Yet, most of us overlook the obvious education gained from our accomplishments, just as we undervalue the learning acquired from errors in judgment.

After years of nurturing and blending a balanced perspective, uncommon sense and the ability to learn from experience, wisdom reveals what is good, right and true. And this is the path a servant leader follows, eschewing self-interest and selfish motivations.

For the servant leader, wisdom is the result of sorting out what works and discarding the rest. It's realizing that insight is helpful, but hindsight is just as important. It's understanding that the years give an outlook that the days and weeks never can.

Wisdom also cautions against taking oneself too seriously, realizing that the fool within us is prepared to go onstage anytime.

Servant Leaders and Radicals

By now, readers should have a pretty good grasp on the qualities and characteristics of servant leaders.

So, it's time to share a few opinions about their opposites—the radicals among us—and why servant leaders and radicals do not and cannot share the same leadership approaches, styles, and philosophies.

The radicals I am referring to exhibit uncompromising attitudes toward people who do not accept their "truths." They also rarely examine the roots of their beliefs or the origins of their attitudes. Their constant hope is to confirm personal biases and prejudices; thus, they become highly selective in what they permit to enter their consciousness. The more committed they are to their narrow range of truths, the more they insulate themselves from the complex world about them. Raising them may place you on their enemy list.

Inability to recognize doubts and live with uncertainties seriously weakens the soul. Reliance on safe answers and intolerance of tough questions indicate the closing down of the soul's opportunity for growth.

Knowledge and reason require no such tempestuous presentations. Noisy bluster and pushy persuasion are used by a radical to conceal a lack of in-depth understanding of the cause being advocated.

Deep in the psyche of a radical is the commitment to censorship. He not only wants to suppress material that threatens his truths, but he also wants to keep others away from information that fails to conform to his narrow ideology. One example of this radicalism is the attacks of the religious right upon public school curricula and library books.

Also deeply imbedded in the psyche of the radical is contempt—for the world in which he lives, for people who disagree with his certainties, for those who promote freedom of thought, for those capable of intelligent reasoning, and for those who do not share his frustrations.

This contempt gives rise to hatred. No matter how religious a radical professes to be, a major driving motivation is the need to hate as well as the need to express that hatred. A common behavior of radicals is to attack viciously those who disagree with them or who stand in the way of achieving their ends. Their highly personalized assaults spring neither from love nor the desire to reach a compromise resolution.

Radicals have great difficulty distinguishing between information and propaganda. What is generally considered information, radicals call propaganda, if it differs from their beliefs.

Rarely does a radical successfully act alone. Disdain requires company. Hatred needs reinforcing. Only through unified action can the radical nullify feelings of inferiority while gaining a sense of worth and self-respect.

Leaders, be wary of radicals and slow to identify with or encourage them. While their focus on causes may be a positive attraction, their narrow, ideological, uncompromising approach will likely turn away or antagonize more moderate supporters while actively distracting you from accomplishing your goals.

They won't furnish you with a barrel of laughs either!

Servant Leaders and Metanoia

It's difficult for me to think about our elected leaders and not think about **metanoia**.

Doesn't that word sound lovely? It sort of drips off the tongue!

Well, really, it's a beautiful and significant Greek word that means turning your life around. It has to do with a fundamental transformation of the mind and heart. It also means repentance and engaging in a spiritual journey.

Now, if you're a political leader reading this, I'd like for you to consider making this word a focus for the remainder of your official days. If you're a person who intends to run for political office, then I urge you pledge allegiance to metanoia.

Here's the essence of what I'm saying.

I think it would be a blessing if politicians renounced their self-serving ways and became true public servants. What a bounteous gift to the citizens of our nation to have them give up the pettiness of partisan politics and concentrate on how they could serve all of their constituents best. What a holy act it would be if they were to turn away from the purgatory of narrow ideologies to the purifying ideal of responsive and responsible servant leadership.

Metanoia!

Indeed, a political paradise might be at hand.

But, to begin this critical transformation, elected officials must first declare, as Pogo did, "We have met the enemy and he is us."

Metanoia!

To become enlightened public servants, officials must renounce the selfish demons and devils within that have gained their attention and, unfortunately, their allegiance.

Metanoia!

To discover the goodness within that will enable them to commit themselves to the common good, they must acknowledge and discard the defense mechanisms that have nurtured and protected their bloated egos.

Metanoia!

Making this necessary, difficult change requires a rare form of courage. To admit the need to repent and adopt new principles, purposes, and goals is no easy assignment. To look deeply inside one's soul and decide to make changes that will launch one's self into a journey that leads to true servanthood requires an openness to new ways of thinking and being, as well as the fortitude to honestly confront the truths and perceptions that one is carrying around. The baggage a person inevitably picks up during a lifetime needs to be consciously examined—such as material goals, self-centered achievement needs, conventional wisdom, societal value priorities, and the role of public servants.

The development of a new consciousness is an individual discipline. But if our political leaders could bring about a collective metanoia—where the courage of each politician encourages others—a communion of selfless public servants might become a reality.

If politicians accept the challenge of metanoia, they would take a giant step toward becoming servant leaders—and a huge step toward making this a better world for our children, grandchildren, and all the other children who will live in the world they inherit from us.

Thoughts on Leadership

Within many people there is at least one critical flaw that prevents them from achieving success. Leaders need to be especially tuned in to discovery and correction.

Leaders, focus on the consequences of your actions and decisions and you will reduce significantly the need to rationalize and make excuses.

What people have in common is their humanity and time. What sets an effective leader apart from others is how well he develops the former and uses the latter.

Leaders should learn to adapt their communication to the receiver and to be sensitive to what language will be understood and accepted by a particular audience. Speaking over people's heads or underestimating their intelligence is equally foolish. Putting yourself in their place is the critical first step in effective communication.

Self-deprecating humor combined with integrity will disarm all but the most belligerent of audiences.

Trying to lead a group without a plan is like turning a business over to most teenagers—the results will be messy and the losses severe.

The Virtue of Change

Once upon a time in an ancient Korean village, a house burned down.

Three chickens inside perished.

While poking around the ashes, villagers came upon the chickens and began sampling the new delicacy.

Intrigued by the taste, a month later they put several more chickens in another house and set it afire.

Six months later, they put a pig in a house and burned it to the ground. The pig provided them another tasty delicacy. The villagers were excited and very pleased with their new culinary discovery.

Over the next few years as villagers torched one house after another to feed themselves, a young man approached the village elders and humbly suggested that an inevitable result of this practice was that soon they would no longer have a village to live in.

"But the people are happy and contented now. What would you have us do?" they asked the young man.

"Why do we have to burn down our houses to roast our chickens and pigs? Why don't we build a fire down by the creek and roast them there?"

Change occurs when someone offers a solution that no longer requires us to destroy houses to roast chickens and pigs.

There is considerable security in believing that what we are doing is right and proper; that the old ways are best.

After all, we assure ourselves, doing things the way we've always done them is comfortable and comforting. We appreciate the music in our lives most when we hear it over and over. Right?

But the flip side of that record is rooted in change. And freedom, in the words of philosopher Sam Keen, involves the awesome decision to "make the future different from the past. If we are not free to change, there is no future to talk about."

Being free enough to select change as the preferred road to the future involves a risk. Moving from a known and comfortable pattern of behavior is a choice fraught with unknowns. It may turn out better or worse. In any event, striking out on one's own will be an adventure.

Which, among other things, means the new road forward will not be boring. Boredom springs from the phrase, "There is nothing new under the sun."

It takes courage to move away from a present that is scripted by the past. We gain confidence when we believe the past provides the models for dealing with new situations. But we gain confidence when we break from the comfortable way of doing things and overcome the difficulties and challenges inherent in change.

The guy who wrote about the "road less traveled" had it right!

Leaders and Change

The Meaning of Change

Leaders are people who have accepted responsibility for bringing about change. Rarely is this not a part of your "job description."

Fortunately, leaders already know a great deal about the subject; you've been dealing with it since birth. So, let's agree you are somewhat of an authority on the subject.

However, in the many years I have been working with leaders, no other topic comes close to being requested as a seminar subject or as an issue to be discussed in consulting sessions. Leaders in business, government, health services, and education frequently ask such questions as: How do we understand change? Why is change so frightening to some people? Why do people resist changes that are in their best interests? Are there concepts and ideas that we can use to initiate positive changes in our organizations?

I once determined that I had conducted seminars on managing change in all but two states during a five-year period. What follows here is a summation of a day-long seminar on the topic, as well as an expansion of a lecture shared with leaders who attended a week-long seminar at The Menninger Foundation back in the mid-seventies when I was Director of Seminars. I'll try to deal as succinctly as possible with the basic psychological principles that govern the dynamics of change. In my experience, what follows will help leaders discover alternatives to mindless resistance and elicit positive responses.

First of all, let's acknowledge that each of us is affected by change in two major ways: we produce change and we're the victims of change. We cause change in others, just as others cause us to change.

To put it bluntly, leaders are up to their necks in change; a major challenge of most people in leadership positions is to initiate change and successfully bring it about.

To deal constructively with change, the first guiding principle is to understand that change causes **stress**. A person may react to change by becoming disoriented or by growing. Regardless of the nature of the change or the abilities of the person to manage a particular transition, the process of change will be a stressful experience in one way or another. Like change, stress is a normal part of human existence.

A corollary of the first principle is that change is also a **risk**. Whenever a person makes a change, he leaves the present structure that has provided a degree of comfort and security. The familiar usually is more comfortable than the unfamiliar. Fortunately, however, human beings are adaptive creatures. Considerable evidence indicates that men and women can make many adaptations in their value systems, their orientation to new situations and environment, and their basic psychological structure. The risk is in confronting an unknown outcome; the challenge is to come to terms with that unknown.

The third and perhaps the most critical principle is to recognize that change involves **loss**. Regardless of the rewards and benefits promised by a change, the change will invariably involve a severance from a previous source of gratification. In early childhood a feeling of loss gives rise to fantasies of fear, abandonment, and pain. A baby reacts to these feelings with an expression of anger; adults are no different. Take a bottle away from a baby and the puzzled look on the baby's face is quickly replaced by a loud, lusty cry of protest as the infant demonstrates rage in every possible way. Since adults have learned that the open expression of anger is somewhat taboo and often elicits retaliation, they usually repress anger and turn it inward. Anger turned into ourselves often leads to depression which appears in a variety of physiological and psychological symptoms.

Here's the key point, leaders: People do not want to make a change unless the rewards and benefits outweigh the stress, risk, and loss.

Factors Influencing the Acceptance or Rejection of Change

The word "change" has many meanings, primarily because the process of change has a number of negative and positive associations accumulated through a lifetime. The acceptance or rejection of change appears to be strongly influenced by the following critical factors:

Attitude. Most people believe that the nature of change itself is the most important factor in its acceptance or rejection. Just as critical, however, is the attitude of the person initiating the change. For this reason, it's important that leaders who attempt to bring about change have an understanding of human behavior.

Attitudes toward a given change will likely be mixed. We may be negative toward a change because it upsets our usual methods of dealing with issues. We may resist because the change threatens our security. At the same time we may have a desire for new experiences because of the benefits that may occur as a result of that change. This period of uncertainty is part of the change process.

If a leader attempting to bring about change is positive about the change, communicates this positive attitude with honesty and without embellishment, and is concerned with the feelings of the people involved, that change is more likely to be accepted than if it were initiated by a leader having a neutral or negative attitude.

Habit. Once established, habits tend to continue regardless of their original purpose. A habit becomes intrinsically satisfying quite apart from its original reason. Thus, change and habit are antagonists. Behavioral habits most often exist because they result in an economy of physical and psychological effort; they prevent us from having to learn new things repeatedly. All of us enjoy the familiarity and security of knowing where something is and how to do something without thinking about it.

> *For example, most men carry their wallet, loose coins, keys, and handkerchief in the same pocket every day. While dressing each morning, they put these items in their pockets without conscious awareness. As the day progresses, they use the items and return them to the same pocket automatically and unconsciously. But if a hole in the pocket occurs and they must reorder items, it's likely they will experience conscious discomfort as the items are placed and carried in an unfamiliar location. Although this is a small change, it's significant enough to cause a disruption of a familiar, personal habit.*

Even patterns of thought become habitual, for we like to know what we think about something without having to reexamine the basic assumptions of a particular belief. The continued popularity of "old wives tales" is one instance of this phenomenon. History is replete with examples; the world is flat, man will never reach the moon, women are biologically inferior to men, Japan will never attack "us."

By the way, leaders, older folks are considered more resistant to change than younger people. Do you know why? As we age, we develop routines. Routines become deeply embedded habits that oppose change and are hard to break. Additionally, older folks may be less motivated than young people to make changes.

Dependence. Closely related to the issue of habit is dependence. Each of us in our earliest days was dependent on someone who determined whether we lived or died. We needed milk and love, and the absence of either would have resulted in our demise. As adults we have not lost these dependency needs despite our frequent efforts to deny their existence.

Intimately tied to dependence is the issue of self-distrust. Children tend to incorporate the values, beliefs, and attitudes of those who care for them. To be "good" they soon learn to do what their parents want or tell them to do, to accept what their parents want them to accept, and to distrust their own impulses if these are at odds with parental communications or instructions.

Even after a period of adolescent rebellion, children or young adults continue to imitate their adult models. For instance, the first time I voted in a national election, I followed the preference of my parents and voted a straight ticket of their political party, essentially a conditioned, non-critical act.

The parroting of behavior is largely caused by the principle of primacy. This principle implies that when an organism copes with a new situation successfully, it develops a pattern that is usually persistent. When something works and is accepted by those around us, that action is tried again. We depend on that behavior. Alternatives are then resisted because of our dependence on established patterns. Frequently we are not even conscious of those patterns in ourselves. Sometimes we are jarred into awareness when confronted by a routine that doesn't work or when we explore a particular behavior response as new patterns are developing.

Remember the story about studying for my first college exam and failing badly? That's an example of my finding it necessary to change a particular behavioral response if I wanted to continue my college career!

Selective Perception and Retention. Each of us prefers to maintain a consistent self-image. To maintain that self-image we often go to great lengths to avoid information that does not "fit" our beliefs or values and to seek information that supports our views. Put differently, we see things not as they are, but as *we* are. Thus, the old cliché "My mind is made up, don't bother me with the facts" is anything but facetious.

The more a person is committed to a course of action, the more that person resists information which threatens her own point of view. We perceive what we wish to perceive, we hear what we want to hear, we believe what we want to believe, and we retain as "fact" information that is consistent with our system of beliefs and values. People in Kansas—a state in which I used to live—who bought homes that had storm cellars or basements were more likely to believe in the eminence of tornadoes than those who didn't have storm cellars or basements.

The Unconscious. To understand the process of change, it's important to recognize the power and influence the unconscious part of our personalities has on our behavior.

From our earliest moments, each of us has had a personal tape recorder operating. Everything we've ever done is on tape, recorded in our unconscious. All of our experiences with people, things, places from the moment of birth now influence our judgments, likes and dislikes, aspirations, ambitions, and ideals. What we do or not do is primarily determined by the unconscious part of our personality.

An awareness of the power of the unconscious explains why we and others resist changes that, on the surface, appear salutary and desirable. Here are a couple of examples:

> ◇ *A man who has experienced a wretched marriage and a bitter divorce believes he would like to remarry because he longs for intimate companionship. Yet he never seems to find the "right" person. Unconsciously, he rejects each potential mate because he fears the marriage might turn out to be like the first one. Or, there may be other powerful unconscious associations operating, such as comparing women with his mother, a fear of close involvement, idealization, or basic inferiority feelings.*

◇ *A woman received a promotion and was transferred to company headquarters in another city. Although initially overjoyed, within six months she was in the the throes of a deep depression. Through therapy, she realized that the promotion was less important to her than the friends she had left, the job she had held, and the community she had come to love. She sought and received her old job back. Consciously she thought she wanted the promotion. Isn't that what all executives want? Unconsciously, the losses she experienced were more than she could handle. The gains were not enough.*

The moral? It's wise to pay attention to the unconscious part of your personality. When we feel forces within tugging at us; notice inner confusion or inexplicable thoughts; have unpleasant dreams or trouble sleeping; experience sudden shifts in our personality, temper outbursts, or a sharp increase in our eating/drinking patterns, it's time to stand back and reconnoiter. The best course may be to seek some honest, gentle feedback either from someone close whom you can trust or from a professional therapist who can help you work through the issues you are struggling with.

Feelings. Locked closely to the unconscious are the feelings we have that influence whether we accept or reject change. Persuasive arguments, critical information, and a wealth of substantive data may be important in influencing a person to accept a change, but these appeals to the intellect are seldom as powerful as the feelings of the person involved. Put succinctly, our reaction to change is more often affected by the heart than by the mind, more by a "gut" response than an intellectual determination.

This point was brought forcefully home to me some years ago when my family prepared for a move to another community:

Our children were then six and eight years old, yet they packed two Mayflower barrels full of old and neglected toys. Adding up the costs mentally, I confronted them with the "facts": 1) The toys were old and no longer used, 2) they surely had outgrown them, 3) other children could better use them if we gave them away, 4) it was going to cost us to move them. Despite my kind, yet firmly persuasive manner and my excellent arguments, I was met with four eyes full of tears. Recognizing defeat, I quickly reconsidered, embraced them, assured both that the toys would indeed accompany us, and left them happily packing another box. Impressed by this new learning experience, I looked for my wife in order to share my insights with her. I found her busily engaged in packing two large boxes with old copies of Better Homes and Gardens *and* Ladies Home Journal. *Exercising more cautious restraint, I inquired gently why "we" were moving the magazines. She replied, "There are articles in them 'we' will want to refer to." I left quickly to pack several large, lovely quartz rocks I found in the yard.*

Clearly, we were cutting our losses. Rational arguments could tell us that these items would likely remain untouched wherever we put them in our new home. But they had become part of us; we cared about them and were unwilling to part with them. The same is true of young children who cling to an old, ragged blanket or a well-worn teddy bear. Attachments to things, like to people, are emotionally based; before altering these attachments, feelings must be considered.

Persuasive arguments, critical information, and supporting data should be marshaled in appropriate situations. Indeed, some changes require this approach. But no matter how much convincing, objective information is applied to the change process, the feelings of the people involved will have to be considered and dealt with.

Surprises. Change often results in anger, and precipitous change is likely to produce an intensely angry response. Even a minor change, suddenly introduced, usually causes a sharp reaction. The more sudden the change, the more acute are the reactions to it. Similarly, a person may internalize a change that is introduced slowly without ever thinking about or being aware of the nature of the change.

> *This was brought to my attention a number of years ago when I was conducting a seminar. Engrossed in my efforts to outline major points on a blackboard, I was surprised and angered when my chalk broke. Before I could control my feelings, a barnyard four-letter word escaped just loudly enough for the first several rows of the audience to hear. Embarrassed, but reassured by their laughter, I offered an apology and continued. Later in the morning as one of the participants was busily taking notes, the lead in his pencil snapped. He, too, made an audible comment—the same obscenity, as a matter of fact. After much laughter, we took time to discuss our very human response to sudden change. We reflected that if the chalk and graphite had simply worn down we would have hardly noticed it. But the surprise of the two breaks, inconsequential as they were, produced quite different reactions.*

Sacrosanct Areas. People tend to reject change when it touches areas of their lives they consider to be ethical, sacred or absolute. Within organizations, change will be resisted when it touches organizational taboos or rituals.

Sacrosanct areas within people and organizations have evolved over a long period of time and have been validated by sacred institutions, by people whose moral values have been influential, and by events that have involved ritualistic or ceremonial elements such as baptisms, marriages, and graduation exercises. These kind of experiences or events have confirmed in people what they should or should not do, believe or not believe, accept or not accept.

Leaders, the suggestion is that you not fool around with sacrosanct areas!

Guidelines for Initiating Change

The complexity of personality prevents the establishment of clear or precise rules of human behavior. It's impossible to provide blueprints to follow when dealing with change. However, there are a few guidelines that should be considered by leaders who are initiating and implementing change within their organizations or groups:

◇ Be aware that people are more likely to accept change when they have been involved in the planning and implementation of that change, when they feel that it is "ours" rather than "theirs."

◇ Be realistic about the advantages and disadvantages when urging people to make a change. It's common for those initiating change to accentuate the rewards and benefits to be gained while ignoring or downplaying the difficulties and losses that will likely occur. It's natural, of course, to dwell on the positive side of change, but the advantages and rewards will not neutralize the negative feelings of loss and resentment. If a change is strongly urged, accompanied by incentives, people may make a change without understanding the pain and losses they will suffer later. Consequently, it's not unusual to note symptomatic and pathologic behavior in people who have been subjected to great change.

In other words, be careful about "selling" a change.

◇ The longer a person or organization has remained attached to the status quo, the more resistance to change will be encountered and the harder it will be to initiate change. It is probable that an extended time will be needed to effect any change. Additionally, it's important that the people affected or involved understand the reasons the change is being initiated.

◇ Be aware that the effects of change are cumulative; they add up! A series of rapid changes often has severe negative results. After a change is initiated, time should be allowed for the change to settle rather than introducing another innovation. This is especially true when there is not a strong attachment to or identification with the leader. People need time to adapt to a change. Don't hit your followers too quickly with another one or you're likely to see a lot of them ducking and cringing when the next shot whistles in!

◇ Finally, an analogy. An elm tree puts down a number of roots into the soil from which it draws the nourishment necessary to sustain life. Cutting off one or even two of the roots of the tree will not seriously affect its life or growth, but if most or all the roots are severed the tree will be seriously damaged or die. Human beings also put down a number of roots (family, home, work, community, church, neighborhood, school) and may respond just as the tree does if most or all are severed.

When a plant is transplanted, it needs time and additional care in order to effectively put its roots down in the soil and gain nourishment. People react in similar ways. After experiencing change a person needs time to become rooted in the new environment in order to gain necessary support. The assistance of others is crucial to successfully and effectively make the transition to a new environment.

Heed the lesson, leaders, aftercare is critical!

Summary On Managing Change

A leader better understands change when recognizing it is stressful, involves risk, and always means loss of some sort. Folks do not want to make a change if the rewards and benefits aren't equal to or greater than the stress, risk, and loss involved.

It is helpful to remember that to successfully initiate change:

- ◇ The attitude of the person initiating the change is as important as the nature of the change itself

- ◇ Some understanding of the unconscious motivation of human behavior is necessary

- ◇ Habit and change form an unhappy marriage

- ◇ The issue of dependence and self-distrust are factors to be considered

- ◇ People function through the principle of selective perception and retention

Remember also, to reduce resistance to change a leader should be aware that:

- ◇ The feelings of the people involved are critical

- ◇ Change introduced slowly is more apt to be successful than precipitous change

- ◇ Incentives and rewards do not neutralize negative feelings of loss and resentment

- ◇ People respond better to change when they are involved in planning and implementing it

- ◇ The longer a status quo position exists, the more resistance will be encountered

- ◇ The effects of change are cumulative

- ◇ Aftercare is important

Leaders, remember that old saw about death and taxes being the only two things you can count on? Feel free to add "change" to that maxim!

Thoughts on Leadership

Leaders, when you find yourself pursuing a wrong course of action or heading down a road that leads nowhere, have the courage to turn around. It's not strength of character that causes you to continue, but stubbornness. Inattentiveness or a bad choice may have put you on the wrong path, but to continue only makes you an obstinate fool.

Try to avoid buying into other person's worries. Rather, help them see that their anxieties are, in truth, concerns or challenges. People who worry constantly often try to recruit folks to become fellow worriers. That's not for you!

An effective leader knows when to pack it in. Most of us have been frustrated with leaders who should have "retired" months, if not years, earlier. If you're uncertain about whether you should continue in your position, ask a few trusted friends—but be sure they are the kind who will tell you what you need to hear, rather than what they believe you want to hear. Knowing when to exit a position gracefully, rather than return for undeserved encores is an important part of a leader's stewardship.

A successful tenure as a leader is the result of wise choices, good judgment, trusting relationships, caring servanthood, important accomplishments, and a pinch of luck. Never underestimate the latter.

A self-promoting leader may find notoriety, but it's a destination only the vain choose to inhabit.

A Lovely Cow

"Oh, what a lovely cow," exclaimed the gentleman from the city. "But why doesn't it have horns?"

"There could be several reasons," replied the rancher. "Some cows don't get horns until they're older. Horns have been removed on others, and some breeds are hornless. This one has no horns because it's a horse."

A person's judgment, of course, is no better than his experience.

That goes double for leaders.

If a leader believes he is leading a herd of horses which, in reality, are cows, he's in a whole heap of trouble.

It's like the wonderful maxim in the great musical comedy, *The Music Man*: "You've got to know the territory."

When a person faces the challenge of leading a group, he had better be prepared. And that means he must find answers to some important questions: Who are these folks? What do I need to learn about them? How much knowledge and experience do they already have on the subject? What do they expect of me? What preparation do I need to do to best serve them?

How many times have you watched someone tackle an assignment—chair a meeting, sit on a panel, make a presentation—and fall flat on their face because they didn't do the homework necessary to make an informed contribution?

Anyone who has attended meetings of elected officials can surely identify those who have read the agenda materials and thought critically about the issues as opposed to those who are trying to fake their way through the discussions.

Effective leaders have an enlightened and heightened sense of responsibility. They understand that when accepting a position of leadership they also have committed themselves to be as informed and as knowledgeable as possible about the people and issues with which they will likely be involved.

One of the fascinating aspects of accepting a position of leadership is that, implicitly and explicitly, trust is involved. Followers trust that their leaders will serve their best interests by equipping themselves with the information and knowledge necessary to render good, if not wise, decisions.

Of course, trust is always a fragile commodity. While it may be extended initially to leaders, it can be lost beyond recovery by one thoughtless encounter, one false statement, or one attempt to mislead those who offered their trust.

So, in the words of the Boy Scouts, "Be Prepared." Leaders will discover that's an imperative to being honest and trustworthy.

Boy Becoming

Once upon a time in a town known far and wide for its quality of life, a boy aspired to become a leader.

He spoke to his father about his dream, who, proud of his son's desire to serve, sent him to a woman possessed not only with considerable wisdom, but with a long and distinguished record of service within the town.

After attending carefully to what the boy told her, she agreed to teach him the basics of leadership.

"What I want you to do," she said, "is to spend a year within the town's boundaries alone, then return here and tell me what you have heard."

When the boy knocked on her door twelve months later, she bid him enter and asked him to describe all that he had heard.

"Ma'am, I heard the winds howling, thunder, the noise of street construction, the horns of automobiles, the voices of walkers, the yells of children, the roar of airplanes, the chirping of crickets and birds, and music from loud radios."

When the youngster had finished, the woman told him to go back into town for another year to listen to what more he could hear.

The boy was puzzled by her request. He believed he had heard every sound clearly and many times.

For weeks and months the boy walked throughout the town and sat through long nights, listening. But he heard no sounds other than those he had heard the first year.

Then one morning, as he sat silently under a tree, he began to discern the gentle whispers of sounds unlike any he had heard before. The greater his attention to the sounds, the clearer they became. Gradually, over the next few weeks and months, a feeling of enlightenment enveloped him.

When the lad returned to the woman, she asked him what he had heard.

"Ma'am, I heard sounds I never heard before. I could hear the unheard—animals conversing silently but clearly, messages sent by the trees and flowers welcoming the rains, and people near me communicating although they were not speaking words."

The woman nodded approvingly. "To become a leader you must learn to hear the unheard. It is truly important for a leader to listen to the hearts of people, and to hear their unspoken feelings, unexpressed pain, and silent cries for help. Only then can a leader understand them and gain their confidence and serve them well.

"You must continue to listen beyond their superficial words if you are to hear their souls speaking to you. It is there that you will hear the truths contained in their feelings, opinions, and desires."

(Adapted from an Oriental parable.)

Thoughts on Leadership

Within every leader's mind should be a place where revisions grow. It's where impressions are modified, judgments are altered, opinions are discarded, truths are invalidated, beliefs are suspended, and where he simply feels free to change his mind.

Nurture the highly contagious generosity of spirit. When it flourishes, friendship and love will also grow.

It is difficult to be vile and mean in the presence of a person of dignity and grace. Try to be that person, leaders.

Leaders, try hard never to give away your control of self. Try to avoid statements such as, "You make me angry!" A more honest statement would be, "I have permitted you to make me angry." No one can assume control over you without your consent. Hold on to your control.

Be creative, leaders, but not in justifying your mistakes. Understand that you are capable of repeated acts of stupidity and personally harmful behavior because of your ability to persuade yourself that the results of your actions will not be consequential.

Effective leaders know it is not necessarily a badge of honor to be regarded as an agreeable person. They understand they are at their best when they disagree with those who promote prejudice, bigotry, hate-mongering, injustice, and greed.

Most leaders have the capability of inflicting pain and suffering. This is an awesome realization. A leader must come to grips with the ramifications of this issue. In every relationship, decisions about the use of power must be considered and made—hopefully with kindness and charity.

A Small Difference

Here's another story from my days at The Menninger Foundation. Some of you recall that Menninger's was a psychiatric/psychological institution encompassing adult and childrens' hospitals, research facility, training center for psychiatrists and psychologists, and the Center for Applied Behavioral Sciences which consulted with organizational leaders and held week-long seminars for business, government, education, and health care leaders.

Our Center staff worked with "well people," which we assumed the leaders were.

And the majority of them were for the most part.

Which is the subject of this short essay. Let me introduce it with a short story.

A young physician on his way to becoming a psychiatrist was interning at a veterans hospital. He was assigned to a ward filled with veterans who were experiencing mental/emotional problems. He spent much of the first year treating approximately twelve of them under the clinical direction of an experienced psychiatrist.

After about eight months, the young intern became uncomfortable with himself and his relationship with the former servicemen. He spent several weeks examining the cause of his discomfort before deciding what was precipitating the problem.

At a weekly session with his supervisor, he said this to him: "Sir, I have been very uncomfortable these past few weeks and I think I now know why. I've concluded that the men I'm treating are no different from me."

His mentor invited him to expand on that thought.

"I don't know how else to say it. They simply don't behave that differently from me, have many of the same thought patterns I do, laugh at what I laugh at, and overall it's increasingly difficult for me to differentiate between them and me!"

The old mentor smiled—he'd heard all this many times before from other interns—and then he asked the young doctor to do what, at the time, seemed very strange to him. "I want you to put your hands in your trouser pockets. What do you feel?"

"My keys," he replied.

The older gentleman smiled again, and then said, "That's right. You're the one with the keys!"

And that was the lesson.

And the difference.

What his mentor was telling the young man was that the line between mental health and mental illness is a small one. The similarities and differences between well people and sick people are often blurred.

I'll never forget the words of the famous psychiatrist, Dr. Will Menninger, who said, "The incidence of mental illness is one in one." In other words, we all act a little crazy at times.

Now, of course, some folks are seriously mentally ill—they need expert treatment and many need to be hospitalized. I'm not talking about the really sick people; I'm talking about the vast majority of us who are walking around, managing life as best we can. But even many of those who are hospitalized appear to function like you and me.

I think leaders need to possess this kind of perspective. Just because they are leaders doesn't make them different from everyone else. There's no need or gain in setting themselves above or apart from others, even those who exhibit strange behavior. I like the "We're-all-in-this-thing-together" approach to others

Dr. Karl Menninger, Will's brother, used to get on the case of psychiatrists and psychologists who labeled patients. He said that once you labeled them—paranoid, schizophrenic, bipolar—you began treating them that way, and the patients and doctors would have a tough time breaking away from the label.

Leaders, let's be careful how we label individuals. Maybe we shouldn't label them at all.

It may be helpful to keep in mind there's only a small difference between us.

Kicking the Pepsi Machine

There are some important behavioral principles that leaders need to understand.

And here's one of them.

How I wish I had appreciated it when I was a youngster. Maybe it would have prevented me from getting into so much trouble—although I really doubt it.

Growing up in the 1930s and 40s in Kansas City, Mo., we didn't have neighborhood gangs—not like today—but we did run around in pretty well-defined groups. Sometimes my buddies and I would stray into an adjacent neighborhood, or more accurately a park, since they were the real centers of youngsters' territory back then, and the local "sentinels" would challenge us.

We'd yell insults, both groups might throw rocks, that to my knowledge never hit anyone because we never got that close to one another. Then we'd swagger back to our turf, exaggerating and romanticizing our perceived triumph. Within a few days, of course, the kids we visited would walk over to our park, and we'd repeat the process.

Then there was the time my best buddy, Bobby Cox, from down the alley, didn't choose me for his Saturday morning football team. That hurt. Until, that is, I was able to provide him with several wrong answers as we studied for the math quiz we took the following Tuesday.

I also remember the time I asked the prettiest girl in the sixth grade, Mary Alice Nelson, to be my special valentine, and meet me at the movies Friday night. She not only refused both entreaties, but told me she didn't even like me. I was miserable until the next afternoon when I slipped a spider under her desk top.

The pitch of her scream shook the class when it crawled up through her empty ink well and even made staying after school that day—and the next week—an acceptable, if not gratifying, penalty.

But the incident that I remember the clearest was when Mrs. Swanson forced me to sing a solo in front of my seventh-grade class. Despite my pleading—for at that age, I was trying hard to be a tough guy to gain the admiration of my buddies—she insisted, and I had to do it.

Of course, she paid for it. The next week I spilled ink on her lesson plans. Convinced that she deserved more punishment and needing to recover my "toughness," I let the air out of one of her automobile tires. Showing off in front of my buddies proved to be a mistake. One of them ratted and they kicked me out of school for a week. Worse, I had to apologize.

Life at home during that week wasn't exactly a whoopee time either.

So, what big principle do all these incidents illustrate?

Lex Talionis! The law of retaliation.

Or, in "Old Testament" terms: an eye for an eye, a tooth for a tooth.

Even little babies are on to it. Take the nipple from the baby before he's ready and you are likely to hear a loud, lusty cry of protest. You can play with him for an hour or so, but offer the nipple again, and he probably will clamp down on it for all he's worth. "You hurt me, Mom, so I'll hurt you," is the message he's sending.

Each of us grows up with our psyches tuned to this major behavioral principle. Even as we mature, it never loses its hold on us completely.

Ever watch a grown man put 75 cents in the soft drink machine, fail to receive a can, then kick the machine?

Ever hear of a politician refusing to vote for a colleague's bill because she failed to vote for his?

The principle operates every day.

A few decades ago, the Iowa Legislature classified the sunflower, the state flower of Kansas, as a noxious weed. A week later, the Kansas Legislature declared the Eastern Goldfinch, Iowa's state bird, a public nuisance. *Lex Talionis!*

The principle is a major factor in international relations. A perceived insult or affront draws a retaliatory statement or comparable insult. Indeed, nations fight wars because of this principle.

"You did it to me, I'll do it to you."

Childish, you say? Inappropriate? Sure, but a very real part of human behavior.

Leaders, watch for it. Understand it. Learn to deal with it as positively as possible. You'll likely see it in action soon. And you probably won't have to look very far.

Thoughts on Leadership

A leader will never have the opportunity to work with a person who isn't flawed. Personal imperfection is a given. But, be aware—those people you are serving will also be working with a flawed leader.

Don't be hesitant to challenge your ignorance. You'll be admired if you are first in line to do so. This will reduce considerably the number in line behind you.

Remember that exaggeration is a form of lying. It should be exorcised from a leader's speech pattern. It distorts truth and leads to distrust.

◇◇◇

When leading a group, keep your eyes and ears wide open to the glories of serendipity.

◇◇◇

A major problem for many elected officials is their tendency to reaffirm one another's worth while paying scant attention to those who elected them. They learn to respond to the excesses of colleagues' applause. Confirmed in their self-importance by associates, they gradually lose sensitivity to and understanding of service to the public.

◇◇◇

Effective leaders place a high priority on brevity and self-effacing wit.

◇◇◇

Those leaders who seek the respect of others understand that wisdom is most often found in contemplative silence. Those who prefer listening to their own words, rather than silence, are unlikely tenants in the house of wisdom.

The Angry Leader

Some years ago while attending a conference in Boston and sitting in my preferred location—the back row—an elegant lady sat down next to me. She carried herself like I always thought a Boston Brahmin would, so that's how I thought of her.

She regally nodded to me, but said not a word, nor looked to the left or right, just sat there with her back rigid and her eyes focused on the panel speakers.

The fourth speaker was a government bureaucrat. If that wasn't enough, he was also pompous, arrogant, and very long-winded. I squirmed and fidgeted but my Brahmin didn't change her haughty expression or even re-cross her legs.

But just after the Washington guy said something like, "One final comment I'd like to make," the Brahmin turned to me and with one short sentence, made the whole morning worthwhile and memorable. What she whispered was, "That man is thoroughly constipated."

Leaving me with that eloquent statement, she departed. Obviously, I've never forgotten her. She gave me a new way of saying what I had been thinking, but of course, I would never have considered sharing my earthy version of the constipated word with such a stately, imposing lady.

Now, if you're looking for me to draw some moral or construct some lesson from the above story, forget it. I just threw it in because I thought you'd enjoy it. And because it occurred at the same conference where, the next day, a leader lost it!

I mean, this guy from Harvard was challenged by several members of the audience about something he said, and he got very red-in-the-face angry and began ranting and raving. Until then, my Brahmin was far and away the highlight of the week; this professor topped her. As a conference leader, he blew it big time! Something a seasoned leader would never do.

But that's not to say leaders won't find themselves up against folks who provoke them and test their tempers. So, here are some common statements we tend to make when angry, along with a few thoughts that may help you manage your anger more positively and constructively.

"You make me angry!" Nope—no one has that kind of power, unless you give it to them. You permit yourself to become angry. Don't blame another person or situation for your anger. You're responsible for it.

"I gave her a good piece of my mind." Maybe you did, but did your hostility serve a productive purpose? Would you and the other person have been better served had you together searched for a creative solution to the disagreement?

"You always do it." Most statements of anger carry distortions like this one. It's unlikely a person *always* does something a certain way. Exaggerations are common when angry, but seldom are true or helpful. Correct the distortions and the anger will likely dissipate, at least to some degree.

"You're not fair." That may be true, but the reality is that what the two of you would regard as fair probably is quite different. Begin with the assumption that the world is neither just nor fair, and that your concept of fairness is unlike anyone else's. Further, be aware that most people believe their actions are fair and they are, from their point of view. Once you relinquish the notion that your concept of fairness is shared by everyone, much of your anger will likely decline or disappear.

"You deserve what you got." Maybe, but most people do not believe they deserve your punishment. Consequently, your anger is unlikely to result in changing their behavior or in making them receptive to further interactions with you. What *is* probable is resentment, if not retaliation, for your attempts to coerce or control them.

"You can't say that to me." How much of your anger is a perceived attack on your self-esteem? Has someone disagreed with you, criticized you, or failed to behave as you desired? Only your own distorted thoughts can cause you to lose self-esteem, so don't blame anyone else. This kind of anger is inappropriate.

"You never do it right." Translated, this usually means, "You didn't do it the way I would have done it." Or, "You didn't per-form according to my expectations." Possibly *your* expectations were unrealistic. You can try to influence another's performance, but to expect that person to do a task the way *you* would do it, is unrealistic.

"I have a right to be angry." This may be true, but are you handling it in a constructive, positive way, such as directing it into riding a bicycle, attacking weeds, meditating, or waxing your car? Or, are you resorting to negative, destructive behavior, such as yelling at the kids, kicking the dog, throwing a glass, or shouting and cursing at colleagues who are challenging you?

If you can, try to take a moment when your anger begins to build to ask yourself if you are allowing the situation or person to pro-voke you unnecessarily. This pause may help you direct your anger into positive channels.

If you can do this, you are well on the way to handling your anger and increasing your effectiveness in disagreeable situations.

A Proud Imperfectionist

It was a boyhood buddy who first taught me a lesson about perfectionism.

Joey and I were doing a school project together. He agreed to begin with the preliminary work and I was to finish it off. The day before it was due on the teacher's desk, I still hadn't received his stuff. The next day, he didn't show for class nor answer my repeated phone calls. The teacher gave us an "F," and the following day I gave Joey a large piece of my mind.

"Why?" I asked, after finally cooling down.

"I just couldn't get it the way I wanted," he replied.

"How did you want it?" I responded with as much restraint as I could muster.

"Perfect," he said. That was my first encounter with a perfectionist. And I didn't like it.

Years later I was consulting with the president of a company who, in my presence, expressed anger at one of his vice-presidents for a particular sentence in a seven-page report. The wording was just a tad awkward, although the meaning was clear.

After the VP left his office, I asked him about his anger. "He should know better than to bring me something that isn't perfect," he replied testily.

"You poor man," I said. We spent most of the afternoon discussing his anger and why I responded as I did.

From that early incident with Joey to the session with the corporate president, I had a number of experiences with perfectionists. Many business leaders I had consulted with fell into that category.

The fact was, I **did** feel sorry for them—and, of course, for those who worked with them as well.

Imagine being locked into a behavioral mode that can never be achieved! It's a recipe for unhappiness, frustration, and guilt if there ever was one.

The ideal behavior for themselves and others is destined to fall short of their expectations. Failure is around very corner.

So, this president and I talked about his "Impossible Dream," and why he held it. In his case, he was conditioned by strong parental expectations. He was still trying to prove himself to his domineering father.

I recall talking with him about my own early "tour of duty" as a budding perfectionist and how I finally decided it just wasn't worth it.

"What did you do?" he asked.

"I decided to become a practicing imperfectionist," I proudly replied. "And I've been much happier ever since."

Let me expand on that a bit, leaders, on the assumption that you might have this perfectionist tendency—or live, or work—with someone who does.

First of all, I continue to rejoice in my acceptance of being an imperfectionist. I am, clearly, an enthusiastic proponent.

I believe everything I do can be done better.

Every idea and thought can be improved on.

Everything I write can be rewritten in a more precise, concise, eloquent form.

Long ago I discovered I was a risk-taker. I like the challenge of breaking new ground, starting projects, taking first steps. Perfection simply isn't in the cards for people who like to initiate things. Rarely will a new idea or program come out in a complete package. It's going to have flaws, stuff that should have been included but was overlooked, deficiencies that need correcting by others who will examine it with different eyes and perspectives. Most new things need to go through an experimental stage. The terms experiment and perfection are unlikely to be found in the same sentence (this one excepted).

The more imperfectionists submit their ideas to public scrutiny, the greater chance there is they will be proved wrong or uninformed or illogical.

But that's the risk each of us takes every time we act or make a decision. We subject ourselves to second guesses and criticism.

What an imperfectionist hopes for is understanding, tolerance, charity and, sometimes, forgiveness.

In attempting to elevate the status of imperfection, am I condoning mediocrity, lesser effort, and average performance?

Not at all. Being an imperfectionist doesn't mean that one doesn't attempt to exert his or her best effort. What it does mean is that we put forth as good an effort as possible within the time constraints, remaining realistic in our expectations.

"It won't be perfect, but it will be the best I can do at this time."

Sadly, too many people—and far too many leaders—are being conditioned to think it is possible to give a 110 percent effort. Or, if they only try harder and longer, they can be the perfect leader, write the perfect report, achieve the perfect marriage, or dance like Fred or Ginger.

Nonsense!

This thinking is potentially self-destructive and dangerous.

There are enough chances for failure and guilt in our lives without setting ourselves up for more!

So, consider, please, the virtue of being imperfectionists.

Put yourselves out there, leaders, with all the bravado of Popeye: "I am what I am and that's all that I am."

Thoughts on Leadership

Those who live with certainties will be more difficult to lead than those who live with doubts.

◇◇◇

The goal of a leader is not to get people to think alike, but to think together.

◇◇◇

Your stature as a leader is enhanced when you accomplish your goals without taking credit for the achievement.

◇◇◇

The lies you hear are not as difficult to counter as the myths people perpetuate.

◇◇◇

Many of the most important decisions leaders make can be resolved by asking what the consequences will be for children.

◇◇◇

The consistency of a leader's values, beliefs, and actions determines his integrity quotient.

◇◇◇

A leader best tempers her self-interest by conscientiously reinforcing her commitment to the common good.

Leaders and Stress

No matter what work we do, where we live, or how we live our lives, we all experience stress. As a leader, you are not immune to its impact and effects. In fact, holding a position of responsibility is stressful in and of itself. People expect more of leaders than they do of other people. The expectations, along with increased visibility, the inherent complexities of leading people, the difficulties in serving the disparate needs of individuals and groups, the personal time demands leaders must juggle, the vagaries of the decision-making process, and the constant choices leaders face in their positions combine to create stress among even the hardiest of leaders.

In this section I hope to help you better understand stress and adapt yourself to it while examining some key approaches to living that may assist you.

In tackling the subject of stress, one soon discovers the paradoxes involved: people need it to live fully, but some can't live with very much of it; it may be pleasant or unpleasant; some people consciously seek it, others try hard to avoid it; stress is critical to accomplishment for some people and thwarts accomplishment for others.

How can the term be defined? What can be said about it with some assurance?

1. Perhaps the clearest definition is that stress is any action or situation that places any physical or psychological demand on a person. (Any position of leadership fits this description!) It's anything that unbalances one's equilibrium.

    Stress and change are irrevocably related. Every change, large or small, causes stress. Change requires an adjustment to a new situation. That adjustment is stress.

Since leaders are, with few exceptions, trying to bring about change in one form or another, it can rightfully be said you are a stress-carrier! So, you get it, and because of your position, you give it to others. It seems to me you better have a pretty good understanding of what it is you're "getting and giving!"

2. Most body systems have a specific response to an assault on the body, such as a headache caused by too much sun or tension due to overwork. Stress is a more general, nonspecific reaction that affects the nervous system response. Stress can make people accident-prone and, in some cases, cause serious ailments.

3. Stress in itself is neither pleasant nor unpleasant. It's our perception of the change and of the consequences of our response to change that determines whether the stressful event or situation is regarded as pleasant or unpleasant.

The following examples illustrate this critical point:

Your son walks into the living room while you and your wife are reading the evening paper. He slaps you on the back and says, "Dad, can I have the keys to the car tonight?" Your response may be, "Are you kidding? The last time I let you use the car, you left it with an empty gas tank and a crease in the fender!" Or you could respond by thinking to yourself, "Great! He'll be out for the evening. My wife and I will have several hours to ourselves. I've got some lovely ideas how we can use the time." So you answer, "Son, I'm happy to let you use the car, but put some gas in it and no creases,"

Or suppose your wife says, "Honey, my mother is coming to visit for the weekend." You may think, "Oh my gosh! I think I'll stay at the office Saturday and arrange a golf game for Sunday." Or you might think, "Great! I'll have the first good meal I've had since the last time she visited."

A third example: The boss says, "Mary, can I see you in my office for a few minutes?" You might wonder, "What does that male chauvinist want now?" On the other hand, you may respond by thinking, "Good! There are several things we need to discuss, including the promotion he hinted at last week."

The effects of stress depend on the intensity of the demand made on the adaptive capacity of the body. A strong dosage of stress—such as being a non-injured passenger in a severe automobile accident—may exhaust a person. A normal kind of activity—like a set of tennis—may produce considerable stress without causing harmful results. Thus, stress is not necessarily damaging.

4. Stress is a condition of human existence. It cannot and should not be avoided. Stress is the mirror image of change; it's a result of change, a condition every human being faces constantly. The stress (change) is neither good nor bad in itself; it's how a person handles it that may cause trouble. Some stress is necessary to well-being, and too little of it may be harmful. **Distress is that part of stress which causes psychological or physical pain or suffering.** Depending on how the accompanying pain or suffering is managed, distress may be minimized or exacerbated.

5. Since stress is a natural and normal part of the human condition, it can only be avoided or terminated by death. Short of death, the least stressful condition is indifference, a response some people find acceptable and others (including, presumably, leaders) do not. To care about someone or something is to reject indifference and subject yourself to stress.

6. The effects of distress are not short-lived. A stressful event leaves its mark, regardless of the time elapsed after the particular event. The death of a spouse, a divorce, or the loss of a job, always impacts our lives.

Adaptability

Stress is the physiological component of adaptability.

And adaptability is one of the primary characteristics of effective leaders. While narrow-minded, rigid leaders exist, they are effective only with like-minded followers.

It's helpful to understand that one's adaptation process begins before birth and continues for the rest of a person's life. Before birth, the adaptive response is present, but is seldom used. From birth on, the physiological adaptive response (stress) is increasingly active, although the mother handles most of the psychological adaptive responses. With development of mobility and speech, the child assumes more of the psychological adaptive load freeing the parents—as they are now responsible for less—for primarily the social and economic adaptive requirements.

In his research on stress, Dr. Hans Selye, the physician who took the word "stress" out of the physics lab and applied it to human behavior, is probably best known for his formulation of the General Adaptation Syndrome (GAS), which describes the response of any living thing to a stressor.

The GAS has three distinct phases: the *alarm reaction,* the *stage of resistance,* and the *stage of exhaustion.* I'll illustrate this by using an example from my past when I was a young tournament tennis player.

As I prepared for a tough tennis match, I noted "butterflies" in my stomach. This *alarm reaction* is truly a call to action; I knew I was going to face a challenge or stimulus strong enough to force me to make an adaptation. Clearly, I was reacting differently than when preparing for a practice session.

During the warm-up I began to feel better. My concentration on the match and my immersion in it contributed to my feeling more relaxed. My nervousness disappeared. In fact, I began to enjoy the situation. The *stage of resistance* had been reached and continued late into the match, depending on my physical condition, the skill of my opponent, and the temperature.

But if it was a tough and long match, my resistance or adaptation to the situation began to wear down. When I tired, my reflexes slowed. I couldn't run or move as quickly as I had earlier in the match, and I began to ache and experience pain. I might even get a cramp. I had reached the *stage of exhaustion*. After a rest, I was able—assuming good physical conditioning—to begin another match. Fortunately, the stage of exhaustion is largely reversible. This is true unless the total organism is exhausted, a situation that could result in death.

Normally, our daily activities are limiting and limited. Seldom do we reach the third stage, although we go through the first two stages frequently. Confronting the first two stages—when doing strenuous work or being exposed to severe cold, for example—may produce concern and worry, but fortunately we become accustomed to most stressors. After prolonged exposure, however, resistance begins to break down and exhaustion sets in.

The most distress-resistant people are those who are flexible in coping with the stresses of life. They are discovering and are continuing to refine the necessary psychological, social, and economic adaptational approaches that give them alternative ways of managing their lives and maintaining their equilibrium. These people may be described as having "staying power." Amid the many forces acting on their lives, they remain balanced, a physiological condition known as homeostasis. To gain balance, persons must be able to expand their potential responses and constrict potential assaults (minimize the damage). They can't achieve balance by "putting their heads in the sand," since that reduces opportunities of finding alternatives. Again, a proliferation of alternatives can be stressful, especially when individuals have not set priorities for their lives.

Value judgments that reduce alternative responses may provide short-term satisfactions and comfort, but may not enable one to examine and cull from a wide range of alternative adaptive responses. (The more closed a person is to exploring adaptational options, the more restricted he or she is in the ability to handle assaults or stress-producing situations.) Remaining closed to adaptational options results in restrictions in the ability to handle assaults or stress-producing situations.

In responding to stress, a person has two basic approaches: to fight or take flight. These two response patterns are discussed in some detail under the section titled, "Leaders and Structure."

A major point is that there are healthy and unhealthy adaptational responses. The task is to determine which is which and, unfortunately, this must be determined anew in each situation; there are no simple formulas.

Those who are not adapting well to stress usually have little interest in self-examination. They also tend to use the coping devices of denial, projection, repression, and regression with some regularity. They find scapegoats to blame, denying they have problems or are causing others to have problems, and they excessively criticize the behavior of other people. In fact, they do whatever is necessary to avoid looking critically at themselves. They constrict the realities they must confront.

The more reality persons can cope with, the more likely they are to find alternative adaptational responses that assist in maintaining balance. The more they restrict opportunities to examine realities, the more they limit their range of responses. Thus, people who are "locked in" to particular ways of meeting new situations usually experience more distress.

Such a person tends to force others to adapt. The statement by the hard-boiled executive, "I don't have problems; I give them," exemplifies this response. The distress of looking inside oneself or having to adapt to stress by undertaking personal change is more than this type of person feels able to handle.

It is not unusual to hear a husband or wife say with reference to their marriage, "We don't have any problems." Translated, this usually means either, "I don't have any, she does!" or "We've got them, but we don't talk about them."

Clearly, living with someone else is one of the greatest causes of stress and distress. The closer a person is to us, the more distress we may feel, for if we love that person we're offering permission to hurt us. No one can cause us more distress than the one we love the most. But who is making the most successful adaptation to life? The person who loves and risks distress, or the person who is indifferent to others and thus risks little chance of feeling distress? There is a third alternative to the feelings of love and the feelings of indifference: the negative feelings of hatred, jealousy, distrust, and the urge for revenge.

Dealing with these feelings is a constant chore. How we cope with them determines whether we will enjoy challenging stress or will suffer distress.

Approaches To Living

Nothing is more important to the persons—and the leaders—who hope to deal positively and constructively with stress than their approach to living which, of course, is determined by their philosophy of life. The complexity of the technological world, stressful as it may be, is not the primary cause of stress; it's us.

We humans have the ability to determine the nature and severity of stressful situations. First, we have, to some extent, the ability to control ourselves and the environment in which we live. If hungry, we can find food; if cold, we can put on additional clothes or seek shelter. Also, people have the ability to anticipate and look ahead. This enables us to prepare for new experiences and situations. The better we anticipate and prepare for a probable future event, the more likely we are to manage the stress.

Having the capacity to anticipate and to control self and environment doesn't mean that we exercise these capabilities efficiently and effectively. Responding appropriately to stress is no simple matter.

Basically, there are three types of stress responses. One is the *emotional* response: reactions such as rage, anger, mild amusement, or uncontrollable laughter. A second response, the *behavioral*, involves the way we carry out a task, relate to another person, or perform under stress. A third type is *physiological*. This kind of stress may cause such ailments as ulcers, headaches, back pains, or heart disease. None of these three responses is totally controllable, but each of us can exercise considerable influence over them. How we approach stressful events and situations is primarily a result of how we approach life.

A person's approach to life is largely determined by needs. Abraham Maslow believed that self-actualization is the highest of a hierarchy of needs. This hierarchy, in an ascending order, includes: physiological, safety, security, belongingness, love, esteem, and self-actualization. According to Maslow, self-actualization is becoming what one is capable of becoming. The climax of self-actualization is "the peak experience," that point at which a person knows and feels authentic elevation as a human being. A peak experience has to be earned. During such an experience, a person realizes that what ought to be, is, and then no longer feels stressed to make it so.

Maslow's emphasis on becoming is closely tied to a basic belief of Dr. Hans Selye. Believing that the laws of nature make it impossible to "love thy neighbor as thyself," Selye urged people to try to "earn thy neighbor's love." He believed that egotism is an essential quality of all living beings and that whenever a choice must be made between loving self and loving others, self-interest will take precedence. Further, he suggested that those who seriously pursue the "love thy neighbor as thyself" dictum recognize they are failing and thus develop inferiority and guilt feelings. Although he didn't reject the value of the principle, he believed it can be adapted to conform with biological laws and still be compatible with religious or political creeds.

Selye's approach recognizes the inherent selfishness of humans while encouraging people to serve others. This is the essence of altruistic egotism: by creating gratitude for our actions, we encourage others to share the wish for our own well-being. On this subject Selye, in his book, *Stress Without Distress*, makes another critical statement:

> *Among all the emotions, those that—more than any others—account for the absence or presence of harmful stress (distress) in human relations are the feelings of gratitude and goodwill and their negative counterparts, hatred and the urge for revenge.*

There also are theologians who suggest that "Love thyself, in *order* that you may love your neighbor" is a more realistic statement to live by than "love they neighbor as thyself." It's unfortunate that so many people are put off by the admonishment to "love self." Psychoanalysts recognize that the quality of selfishness is basic to the personality. The Id is that part of a personality which says, in effect, "I want and I want it now!" A baby's personality is mostly Id. People do not lose the Id as they age; however, it may be modified and brought under control by the Superego (conscience) and the Ego, that part of the personality that is in contact with the environment.

The Ego attempts to balance the Id and the Superego. Stress, and certainly distress, occurs as the powerful drives of the Id and Superego (I must and I must not) vie for control. The Ego (I will or I will not) has a big job—it must deal with the inevitable stresses from outside (the environment) and inside (the Id and Superego). The better the Ego balances the many forces impacting the personality, the less distress is experienced. Distress is a response to a troubled Ego—an Ego experiencing difficulty handling conflicting forces.

This sketchy description of personality functioning may seem strange in a section dealing with approaches to living until one understands that *every* element of life is personal, unique, and thus based on each individual's assessment of needs, interests, abilities, and goals. Accurate self-examination should begin with an understanding of why we are as we are and why we behave as we behave. This brief description of personality functioning is intended to provoke a more thorough examination by leaders of personality development, which is a key to one's philosophy of life.

There's a good reason for this emphasis. People who are most susceptible to stress disease, like ulcers and headaches, tend to be first, afraid of their emotions, especially anger, hostility, and aggressive feelings; and second, failing in life in one way or another. A person fearful of anger, hostility, and aggression is likely to try to hide or contain these powerful emotions, which when turned inward, results in susceptibility to depression. The crucial factor in dealing with depression is how one handles it. Everyone is depressed from time to time; a day or two of being depressed is not a great problem. But if a person is depressed for two or three weeks or months, there clearly is a problem that may lead to ulcers, pains, or even a more serious illness.

The individual who is failing in life is also susceptible to stress. Such a person may be highly successful in his or her profession, yet be unsuccessful with marriage, health, or children. A common behavioral ploy of the failing person is to rationalize or compensate by blaming others (projection), to reject criticism, evaluation, or feedback (denial), or to try to live out the void or non-developed parts of life through children (compensation). All too often we see this latter behavior exhibited by parents attending sports events in which their children participate.

Briefly, then, a person's approach to self determines his approach to others and the world in which he lives. The more open to self-understanding, the more likely one is to live a life in which stress is controlled and distress is managed without unnecessary suffering and pain.

To develop a fulfilling philosophy, a person must examine his life in order to determine the stress levels at which he is most comfortable. People who cannot engage in critical and honest self-examination will probably not succeed in finding ways of reducing stress or the anxiety of stressful situations.

Here are additional suggestions that relate specifically to improving one's ability to handle stress and minimize distress.

Establish a relationship with at least one person who will give you open, honest, yet kind feedback about yourself. Self-examination is a requisite first step, but to move beyond our natural tendency to protect our tender spots, we need someone to help us see ourselves as others see us. This person may be a spouse, confidant, or mental health professional.

Seek to better understand the laws of nature. In so doing, you will likely gain respect for simplicity of lifestyle and will tend to experience again wonder and curiosity about the world in which we live.

Try to understand that you should strive to succeed in whatever you do; few things reduce stress as much as success. But be aware, however, that perfection is an unattainable ideal. In pursuit of a cause or goal, strive for what is achievable. To reduce the inevitable frustration that may result from any endeavor, first determine whether the task is really worth working toward; that the frustration, stress, and distress are worth the effort.

Recognize that we live in a world of diversity. Treat people as unique individuals, understanding that there are no truths, answers, and solutions applicable to everyone.

Try to determine the patterns you use to manage stress. How do you usually meet stressful situations? Try to be flexible and adaptive when handling stress. The more adaptive you are, the greater your chances for success and for the reduction of stress and anxiety.

Attempt to develop a variety of ways to gratify yourself. An "all my eggs in one basket" approach often results in an empty basket. People who devote all their primary energies to their jobs, for instance, not only cause problems for their families, but also frequently are unable to cope with situations such as illness, vacations, and retirement. One of the best ways to minimize stress and distress is to select environments—recreational, work, social—that are compatible with one's preferences. A person is happier when engaging in chosen activities.

Each day plan some idleness or times for relaxation. Put your feet up and try to think beautiful thoughts unrelated to work. Or, if you are dealing with considerable stress, practice transcendental meditation or yoga, or other relaxation approaches.

Seek opportunities for personal enrichment such as enjoying art, music, poetry, walking in the woods, tennis, golf, swimming or boating. Hobbies and interests that provoke a change of pace are important.

Consider any day lost that does not contain something of memorable value. At the close of a day, a person should be able to remember at least one event or situation during the day that was good or beautiful—something you don't want to forget.

Understand that a positive approach toward life produces more success and happiness than a negative approach.

Zest in living and working is a mark of emotional stability. Thinking about pleasant things is a lot more fun than thinking about unpleasant things. Without being simplistic, try to focus on the many positives in your life—for example, your family, home, friends, health, or reputation. There is considerable truth in the principle of the self-fulfilling prophecy: We are who we wish to be, we achieve what we want to achieve, we succeed when we believe we will. Our relationship to our self mirrors our relationship with others. A mark of emotional maturity is the capacity to relate consistently to others in a manner that provides mutual satisfaction and help.

Finally, no approach to living can be of value to self or others unless it rests on love. It's impossible to love others without seeing oneself as a person of worth and value. To do this one must develop self-esteem—a critical ingredient. When viewing oneself positively, it is possible to help others in ways that are not demeaning, controlling, condescending, or patronizing. To love is to care, and this should be the hallmark of every relationship we have with others. Not to love and care, leaders, can lead only to the isolation of indifference and the distress of not being loved in return.

Thoughts on Leadership

Leaders, if you don't suffer fools gladly, I suggest you not run for public office.

Life is, of course, a journey. But for a servant–leader, it's also a pilgrimage.

Effective leaders see themselves through their own eyes rather than somebody else's. This is a recognition that their self–assessments are more important than those of others. This doesn't imply they no longer care what others think about them; only that they are more trusting of their own interpretations of who they are.

Leaders should be aware that one of the worst characteristics of power is that it emboldens those who hold it to define reality for those who don't. In time, there is a strong tendency for the power-less to accept the definition of reality put forth by those with power.

Among the most virtuous of persons are those who possess power and don't abuse it.

A wise leader knows that all things do not come to those who wait. It's a lot more realistic to believe that everything comes to her who takes advantage of her time while she waits.

The Flawed Follower and the Leader

"I'll tell you something, Ron, she has unlimited opportunities for growth."

"Why?" I asked my friend, Tom, who was one of the finest leaders I ever met.

"Because she has so many flaws."

"Ample room for self-improvement, you believe?"

"More than ample, but it won't happen, I'm sorry to say."

"Why not, Tom?"

"She's a committed blamer. Her preferred defenses are denial and projection. She makes mistakes, covers her blunders with denials, then projects blame on everyone around her."

"As far as she's concerned, she's blameless. Right?"

"Yep. You familiar with people like that?"

"I'm afraid so. Denials are surrounded with self-righteous accusations and even sanctimonious pronouncements about their own upstanding behavior."

"Well, that's her modus operandi for sure. She has made personal attacks on those close to her as well as strangers who choose to comment critically upon her actions. She believes those who do not buy into her arguments and are rash enough to disagree should be punished."

"I suppose you've tried to reason with her."

"Yes, but it doesn't work. My experience is that people who are into denial and projecting blame onto others do not respond positively to reason. They tend to prefer unreason. Listen to their arguments and you may see how unreasonable and illogical they are. And you know that whenever unreason is countered by reason, the individual using unreason will probably win the argument."

"Explain that."

"Think of a prize fight. If one participant is forced to fight fairly, with gloves on, and to follow the rules while the other person is free to fight unfairly—no gloves, and allowed to kick, gouge, bite, whatever—who's likely to win?"

"So, what do you do? You care about her, but I can understand your frustration with her denials and her attacks on you and others in the group."

"I'm sure you understand she needs professional help. In the meantime, I'll try to relate to her as best I can and hope for that precious moment when she acknowledges her inability to cope with life on her terms. I need to be there for her then."

The Reluctant Leader

He describes himself as "cautious."

His favorite words are "maybe" and "perhaps." His most frequently used phrases are "I'll look into it" and "Let me think about that."

"I weigh things. I don't like to jump too quickly. It's my nature to be contemplative."

That's how he sees himself.

How is he seen by others?

"He doesn't contemplate, he procrastinates."

"He won't take a stand on anything. He hates to make a decision."

"He desperately wants everyone to like him."

The man in question sees himself as a community leader. People who associate with him don't see him that way at all.

What they see is his strong need to be liked and his consequent avoidance of making decisions which may threaten his perceived popularity. He does this by automatically entering into a "flight pattern" when facing conflict or personal confrontation.

When coping with stress, each of us responds with either a fight or flight reaction. We attack or run away. It's pure animal behavior. When threatened, an animal will take on the challenge or turn tail. We humans behave in the same way.

If we are reasonably adaptable, we evaluate each decision requiring action, and either confront it or avoid dealing with it. Each day we incorporate into our behavior a number of fight/flight responses.

Maladaptive behavior occurs when a person's automatic response is consistently in either a fight or flight pattern. The section of this book, "Leader and Structure," provides more information on this pattern of behavior.

The problem facing the public servant is that he is required to make decisions, almost all of which are stressful because they are likely to alienate some people. Seeking to be liked by everyone, he uses three flight pattern responses: he delays, hoping the problem will go away; he maneuvers to get other public officials to take the lead and heat; and he blames outside forces—like the media—for exposing his indecisiveness.

The fact is, effective leadership requires a fight response most of the time. Leaders must tackle tough issues, take difficult stands, make unpopular decisions, and risk alienating people when necessary.

But a fight response should not become a pattern. There are times when contemplation and delay are necessary. Which is why leaders should be adaptable, knowing when to retreat and when to push forward.

And they need to understand that being respected is far more important than being liked. If the latter is more critical to them, they should not seek leadership positions.

Thoughts on Leadership

Self-confidence flourishes when nurtured and reinforced. It seldom grows in isolation or without considerable praise and approval. Leaders, try to cultivate caring friends who attend to your well-being and support you as you carry out leadership responsibilities.

The development of critical thinking is essential if one is to become an effective leader. This skill begins with questions, is constructed on disagreement and frustration, and achieves conclusion through thoughtful judgment. To become adept at critical thinking, a leader should learn to tolerate discontinuity, detachment and confusion. Without perseverance, efforts to become a critical thinker will end prematurely.

Never, ever, exhibit moral superiority; it's a clear indication of moral weakness.

Never, ever, come across as self-righteous. Within this type of person— sometimes carefully concealed—is envy, jealousy, and arrogance.

Be cautious, leaders, in carrying around excessively high goals for yourself. Too frequently this translates into also expecting others to hold similarly high goals. Unrealistically elevated self-expectations may result in occasional victory, but mostly disappointments. Excessively high expectations for others often leads them to anger, continual distress, and disillusionment.

Susan and the Mountain

Once upon a time, in a beautiful mountainous area of a western state, lived a young woman who desired to make a positive difference in society. Susan wanted to become a community leader.

For a number of years she met twice-monthly with her mentor, a lady in her seventies who lived on top of the highest mountain in the area. Susan always looked forward to meeting with the wise old lady and took great pleasure in the long walk up and down the mountain.

But in recent months, she began doubting whether she would become an effective leader. Despite having made important contributions within the community that lay at the base of the mountain, Susan felt she had reached a plateau and could progress no further. She recognized that she was an effective leader, but now believed that the wisdom required to help others in significant ways was beyond her understanding.

She decided to share her concern with her beloved mentor. But before she could speak, the old lady said that she had decided to accompany Susan on her walk down the mountain and they would begin the hike now.

As they stood together on the porch overlooking the vastness surrounding the mountain top, the lady asked Susan what she saw. "I see the sun high above us, the hills and mountains around us, and the lakes and town below us."

The lady smiled at Susan's response and they began the long descent.

Halfway down the mountain, the old lady again asked Susan what she saw. "I see several boats on the lakes, a large meadow with flowers, cows asleep near the red barn, and children scampering through streets of the town."

Silently they continued their walk until they were almost to the town. Bidding Susan to sit with her under a large maple tree, the old lady asked Susan what she had learned today, followed by the comment, "Perhaps this is the last time I shall ask questions of you."

Silence was Susan's only response.

After several minutes, the old lady spoke softly and slowly these words: "The road to enlightenment is like the journey we just made down the mountain. We must comprehend that what we see at the top is not what we see part way down or at the bottom. Without this understanding we close our minds to all that we cannot view from our position and thus limit our ability to learn and grow.

"But with this wisdom, Susan, there comes an awakening, for upon reflection we begin to appreciate that alone one's viewpoint is quite limited. You cannot see from one perspective what can be seen from a different part of the mountain."

When her mentor stopped speaking, Susan turned to watch the sun setting over her community. She did not see the old lady begin her trek back up the mountain. But she looked differently at the town—and herself—from that day forward. She knew now, that in time, she would become not just an effective leader, but a significant one.

(Adapted from an Oriental parable)

Childish Behavior

Most of us learn to tolerate the childish behavior of youngsters.

We know their actions will be silly and outrageous at times but realize that is simply part of the growing up process.

Our tolerance is appropriate. We bear with them.

But this same tolerance, when extended to the childish or repugnant behavior of adults, may be inappropriate. Too many leaders haven't figured this out.

How many meetings have you attended where a person dominates by asking a series of far-fetched questions, or harangues the group over nit-picking details, or interrupts with tangential opinions, or insults people by assuming a self-appointed superiority while pointing out the deficiencies of the organization?

The leader does nothing while the members sit quietly, seething with repressed anger, but not wanting to appear intolerant of the perpetrator.

A few years ago I was conducting a seminar in which a young man dominated the discussions. He wanted the other participants to be impressed with his "superior" intelligence and quickness in grasping the essence of the material. By the first coffee break he had become downright obnoxious.

At the break I spoke with him about the need to let others have equal time and how helpful it would be if he would become more of a listener. His reaction was belligerent as he explained that he didn't believe he could learn anything from the other participants and that he intended to continue expressing his point of view in whatever way he wanted.

I quickly escorted him to the registration table, had his seminar fee returned to him, and told him to leave the conference. Which he angrily did.

I was willing to recognize his special need to be the "expert," but I was unwilling to permit his needs to supersede those of the other sixty participants.

While we may tolerate the special interests of individual members of an organization or group, a leader has a larger responsibility to acknowledge the higher interests of the entire membership. The welfare of the participants is more crucial than the needs of an individual member.

Let a member dominate and the silent voices—whose needs may be as great, or greater—will not be heard.

The fact is, leaders often condone dysfunctional people in groups because of their conditioning to be tolerant. They somehow believe they must listen to them even when they disrupt meetings and drive good, quiet people away from the group. They are reluctant or unwilling to ask disruptive individuals to either change their ways, or leave.

In one organization I'm familiar with, a man challenged the printed rules of conduct. He knew he was wrong but enlisted others to support him. It is doubtful he had thought through the effects of his mischief on the future of the organization. Fortunately, the governing board held firm, in effect, telling him and his cronies that the organization was more important than he.

While a leader can acknowledge that each individual is important, there are times when disruptive persons sap energies and diminish the overall purpose of the group. They are unable or unwilling to subjugate their needs to the higher good of the many.

Leaders should respect these people but should not tolerate their behavior.

They have lessons to learn about being a contributing member of a group.

And leaders should see to it that they learn those lessons.

Thoughts on Leadership

Leaders need to guide with passion. But be aware that, in excess, it may be a danger to self, others and life.

Is there a more important skill for a leader to develop than choosing well? Her quality of life might be best evaluated by the choices she makes.

Leaders, don't be seduced by applause when you begin a task and don't expect an encore. If winning the applause of others is a major goal, there will never be enough.

Learn to be parsimonious with words. Over-talking diminishes attention and respect. Speak succinctly with clarity and the praise will roll in.

If you place a high priority on gaining the esteem of others, you are unlikely to succeed. If being yourself doesn't gain their respect, then improve yourself.

◇◇◇

Only a fool is self-satisfied. A wise leader is never completely satisfied with himself, his accomplishments, or the quality of his life.

A Boy, a Dog, and a Life

"I know just how you feel."

Ever had someone say that to you?

Do you recall thinking, and perhaps responding, "No you don't. You couldn't possibly know. You're not me!"

Maybe most of us have had this kind of conversation. We're suffering from an illness or injury and someone tells us he knows how we feel, and then compounds our misery by sharing with us (in boring detail, usually) how much pain he suffered during some previous ailment.

Contrast that with: "You know, I can't possibly comprehend how you feel. If you could tell me, perhaps I could be of assistance."

I resonate with those exchanges. There were three in my earlier years I recall vividly.

I was eight or nine and the dentist extracted five of my baby teeth. I remember emerging from the ether and repeatedly vomiting into a sack as we drove home. My dad laid that sympathetic line on me and I angrily responded, "No you don't. You couldn't…"

When I was in high school, I got out of bed to answer the phone, and explained to the caller that I had the flu. She told me at great length about her recent bout with the bug. It didn't make me feel better.

The third exchange took place while I was stationed in Korea. I was on duty when suddenly I keeled over. A friend next to me called the commanding officer who was nearby. When I came to, he was leaning over me. I can't recall what I mumbled in response to his question, but I will never forget his reply. "You've had a tough day. Let me know if there's anything I can do for you."

At the heart of a meaningful response to pain or suffering is **empathy**. Empathy means understanding and appreciating what's going on within a person. The essence is the Native American maxim that you can't really understand a person until you walk several miles in his moccasins. It's an intuitive connection that some people inherently possess, while other folks have to consciously work to achieve it.

What it isn't is warm fuzzies or glib, meaningless assurance that all is well when it isn't. Empathy means sincerely trying to put yourself in the other's place—in their circumstance at that moment.

So, leaders, want to improve your relationships with people?

Work on developing empathy.

If you can try to understand what your followers are thinking and feeling, you are well on your way to strengthening and solidifying your position of leadership. You gain considerable respect when you take the time and make the effort to appreciate who each of your followers is and what he is going through.

Years ago I discovered a story that brought this message home to me. The author is unknown. But she or he described empathy as well as it can be done, in my opinion. See if you agree.

This is the story of a man who put up a sign, "Puppies for sale." He no sooner had the sign up than there was a small boy standing by wanting to know how much the puppies were going to cost.

The man told him that since they were pretty good dogs he did not expect to let any of them go for less than $25. With a look of disappointment on his face, the youngster asked if he could see them.

The man called, "Lady," and whistled. Out of the kennel and down the runway came "Lady" with five little balls of fur rolling along behind her; one lagged considerably.

The boy spotted the lagger and asked, "What is wrong with him?" The man said, "Well, the veterinarian has examined him and he says there is no hip socket in his right hip. The dog will live, but he'll never be much of a dog."

"That is the one I want to buy," replied the youngster. "I will give you all that I have right now, two dollars and eighty-seven cents, and pay you fifty cents a month until I get him paid for."

The man shook his head, "No, we will make a deal all right, but you don't want that dog. He will never be able to run, jump, and play with you. You want one of the other dogs."

The youngster very slowly pulled up his little trousers. There was a brace running up both sides of his leg, a leather kneecap, and a badly twisted leg. The youngster said, "You know, I don't run so well myself, and he'll need someone that understands him."

Well, it's just a story, but you get the picture. How important it is to try to understand another person, and then develop the ability to put yourself in his place.

The Priority of Listening to Self

Here's another conversation with my friend Tom.

"So much of your time, Tom, is devoted to serving others and working within the community. How do you take care of your own needs?"

"First of all, I try to blend personal life with my involvement in the community. Who I am and what I do within the community flows directly from who I am in solitude."

"Can you explain that?"

"Unless I carefully listen to the messages rolling around within my inner self, I will be a poor respondent to the revelations produced through my interactions with others. Being alone and reflecting upon what I've heard and learned within the community is an imperative step toward maximizing the contributions I might make in service."

"I think I understand, but could you say a bit more?"

"Anytime I immerse myself in the lives of others, I risk losing myself. I can become so wrapped up in the desperateness of lives and the agitation within the community that I may lose perspective and worse, lose the core of my own being."

"Go on."

"Unless I examine my perceptions about life outside myself and reevaluate my own values and attitudes in relation to those perceptions, I risk seeing only the fragmentation of life. I may lose the ability to visualize harmony or construct a balance for my actions.

You see, being alone with myself doesn't mean I have abandoned my external commitments, only that I need to bind my efforts to the source of that service."

"You mean to your values?"

"Yes. There are times when I get so wrapped up in simply doing that I lose perspective on why I'm doing. When I sense this occurring, I realize that I may be trying to escape from something or for some reason I am not at home with myself."

"So you retreat to solitude in order to listen to yourself?"

"Exactly. Unless I effectively renew my engine by listening to myself, I can't listen to others. Unless my self is in order or balanced, I hear from others only what I want to hear."

"Why?"

"Because my own needs are more important than the needs of others. When out of balance, I am so engaged seeking answers to my needs that I can't hear those put forth by other people."

"I suppose many politicians are good examples of persons who cannot listen to others because their own lives are amiss."

"Not only politicians. Many who serve within their communities can't effectively hear what others are saying because they have lost the ability to listen honestly to the voices within themselves."

"How does this happen?"

"The voice of public service is often seductive. It tempts us to function outside ourselves, to let others speak for us, and to live an existence in which our inner voices are subdued by powerful external forces. Our values and morals can be subverted or ignored unless frequently examined and reinforced."

"Which means taking time to be alone and contemplate what's important and right?"

"Yes. Each of us needs an anchor. For me, it's self. I will pull that anchor up and set a course of action only when I feel that my inner and outer selves are in harmony. Then I am reasonably assured that what I do will be consistent with who I am. That means, of course, that I will be serving and acting with integrity."

Thoughts on Leadership

Leaders accumulate a variety of playing cards through the years. Knowing which ones to play at a given time is a sign of good judgment. Knowing which ones and when to discard is a sign of prudence. Knowing which ones to hold, and in what order, is a sign of wisdom.

Leaders who regard HONOR as a key component in all decisions and actions will, of course, experience occasional disappointment, but mostly their endeavors will be filled with serendipitous rewards and unanticipated successes.

In any leadership position, be wary of chameleons. There are people who alter their personalities, beliefs, and opinions to fit or manipulate whatever circumstances they encounter. There is no center to their being and no consistent focus to their actions. They lack integrity. Be slow to invest in them.

Want to be a successful leader? Cultivate tenacity and sagacity.

The intensity of a person's actions has both qualitative and quantitative characteristics. Excellence resides in the former, fatigue in the latter.

To better understand another individual, learn what or whom he worships. Is it self, power, pleasure, fame, wealth, family, job, God? When you discover a person's dominating passion, you get a handle on the motivations that control his behavior.

A leader has ample opportunity to gather clues and insight about her behavior. When favorable feedback occurs, try to hold vanity in check; the unfavorable merits at least equal attention.

Leaders and Structure

What Is Structure? What Is Support?

Most people, including leaders, underestimate their need for structure.

My hope is that anyone who reads this section won't make that mistake again.

You see, structure is the glue that holds an individual together. It's also what holds organizations, groups, armies, communities, and nations together.

But I won't be writing about those bigger entities; the subject is individual leaders and those who aspire to be.

So, here's the primary definition of structure from a psychological standpoint: *STRUCTURE IS SUPPORT!*

To provide structure is to provide support. You and I structure certain things into our lives—in my case, casual sports wear, western art, books, classical music—because we feel supported when we have them near. When we feel supported, we can grow and develop.

Parents usually know to give children clear and firm structure. Children must learn what they can and cannot, should and should not, do. Structure frees children to grow and develop their abilities. Structure tells them that someone cares; it supports them.

Effective leaders understand that if they don't provide people in their organization or group a clear structure, they run the risk of getting little accomplished or even that chaos may develop.

What is *support*? To support means to bear or hold up, to maintain, to aid, to strengthen, to comfort. Support may also be defined as that which provides courage under trial or affliction.

Support may be a concrete foundation buttressing a house, or a $100,000 grant that financially backs or sustains a day-care center, or a prompter who keeps actors on script. We associate support with form, structure, and limits.

One thing support is *not:* sentimental reassurances. These are often the least supportive things you can do for someone, because you are denying their concern. For example, you tell me you're hurting or suffering and I reply that you look fine, everything will turn out all right, and you just need to stop worrying or thinking about it. I am not hearing you at all; I am denying your reality and providing you with zero support. Sentimental reassurances most often are a subtle way of telling someone to "bug off."

When you seek support and receive little or none, you become confused and disoriented. You begin to wonder if something is wrong with your *self,* your being, your identity. This is one of the worst of all possible confusions. Having the self shaken is like experiencing a high Richter-scale earthquake.

We feel supported when we know who we are. To understand ourselves, we need firm structures that reaffirm our identities and, thus, support us. *Support is structure that can be trusted.*

Structure basically means to build, to put together interdependent parts into an organized whole. Arranging elements into a pattern causes the whole to make sense. Structure gives form and meaning to things and to people. Without structure, humans would have a difficult time functioning and surviving.

The universe is structured. Every entity exists in its own unique, individualistic way as part of that universal structure.

Biology and philosophy, dissimilar in so many ways, both consider structure as one of the two defining properties of matter.

Without structure, the world would appear chaotic and bewildering. At times, when we are caught up in the complexities of our lives, it seems impossible to comprehend patterns and structures. In these moments, it's difficult to find meaning in our lives.

It is precisely at these times that we can pull back and take refuge in comforting structures, like home, family, and hobbies. We usually discover that any of these structures can help organize experience and enable us to make sense of things.

Structure gives us at least the illusion of predictability. Without structure, we indeed feel lost.

Fortunately, people seek structure even though they may lose some of the serendipitous richness of their environment by imposing a structure on it.

Sources of Structure

There are three sources of structure: physical, environmental, and psychological. Although I'll focus mainly on the third, it's important to acknowledge the importance of the first two.

Physical

My body is the physical structure that tells me I'm me. Around a skeleton of bones a skin holds together an intricate, complex set of systems. It's a marvelous structure that protects me, nourishes me, and directs me—in mysterious ways at times.

Usually, its signals are clear and simple. When I eat too much or too little, it punishes me. When I push it too hard, it makes me rest. When I abuse my body with unhealthy food or chemicals, it functions poorly. When I exercise properly and eat balanced, nutritious meals, it rewards me.

It's the vehicle I use to deal with the world. Everything I know and experience is channeled through it. By observing my body, others receive the messages I convey, both verbally and non-verbally.

Physically healthy people put a high priority on an integrated, well functioning body structure. Years ago I traveled the country competing in tennis tournaments. To play well, I needed a body that would perform at the highest levels of efficiency, so I took excellent care of it. In later years, I paid less attention to its functioning. It responded by becoming less efficient. Illnesses were more frequent. I became frustrated with my body and condition. More recently I took control again. I exercise regularly, eat nutritiously, and listen diligently to the messages my body gives me. Consequently, the physical part of this entity called Ron Barnes is structurally more sound, dependable and manageable than in my middle years. The body structure is more supportive. The better it works, the better it supports me in my daily activities.

A well functioning body structure results not only in an improved psychological structure but also in an enhanced interaction with the environmental structure.

Environmental

Take a moment and consider the environmental structure surrounding you at this moment. I am most comfortable when surrounded by western paintings, Indian rugs, and classical music from NPR—an environment compatible with my self-concept. When the structure of my environment reinforces who I believe I am and is consistent with my physical and psychological structures, I feel good and at peace with myself.

Most problems we experience in physical and psychological structure originate with our social environment—neighbors, the organization we work in, colleagues, customs, traditions, church, groups we belong to.

Environmental structure also can be physical, and can be frightfully apparent at times. This year a series of hurricanes devastated several states, causing extensive property damage, injuries, and deaths. In my state, we've had severe wildfires for the past several years. Many inhabitants lost their homes. In finding new homes, they had to call on structural sources (family, friends, church, and community, state and national resources) to rebuild their lives and recover from these terrible disasters.

Less apparent than hurricanes and wildfires are the environmental structures we rely on daily: the air we breathe, the water we drink, the land we walk on. When air becomes polluted, water gets contaminated, or the earth quakes or burns, we inevitably become anxious and concerned.

Psychological
The third source of structure in our lives deserves more attention because it's often the least obvious and most undervalued. It's the invisible psychological structure we call "self"—the mind, personality, desires, passions, impulses, needs, moral code, values, reasoning, ability to adapt, memory, perception, ability to test reality, and capacity to integrate experiences into patterns of behavior.

Within ourselves all these forces contribute to deciding how we control our actions. Sometimes these forces are compatible, enabling us to reach swift and confident decisions. Sometimes they are in conflict and pull us apart.

When our psychological structure is harmonious—the forces are compatibly integrated—we appear to others as a well-structured person. We seem well-organized in our activities. We move through on-time schedules. We live by socially approved rules. We know where things are because they are where they should be. We know where we are going—at this moment, on this day, in this year, in life.

Perhaps for some readers I have carried this structure issue too far. Probably most people would like a less rigid set of guidelines. Structure, like most everything else, can be carried to an extreme—to the point of becoming obsessive-compulsive in pursuit of the ideal psychological structure for self.

But the other extreme—no structure at all—is even less desirable. Most of us spend our lives somewhere in the middle; between a rigid, absolute structure and a complete dearth of structure. Buffeted by a myriad of forces, we appear well-structured at times and loosely put together other times.

Psychological structure organizes our ventures and places them in a context for making sense of them. As we sort through various choices, we attempt to integrate them into our physical and environmental structures. In this manner we gain some predictability in our lives.

Consistency can be achieved only when all three sources of structure—physical, environmental, and psychological—are reasonably well-integrated.

Sources of Psychological Structure

We develop our psychological structure on three bases. First, the *people* who tell us what to do. From parents, to older brothers and sisters, to teachers, religious leaders, police officers, and managers, people tell us what we can and cannot, should and should not, do. With each set of instructions or guidelines we accept, we assimilate our identity.

However, as we define our self, we may confuse a role with self. For example, a manager may function at home as a manager instead of a husband or father. Or a mother may operate in a business setting as a mother instead of a manager. When we let a particular role define our identity, we risk losing self.

Second, we get psychological structure from *concepts*. Examples abound: "Love thy neighbor." "Do unto others as you would have others do unto you." "The bottom line." "Natural law." "The Scout Oath." "The Ten Commandments."

These statements and abstractions provide guidance and, to a greater or lesser degree, make our experiences understandable by telling us what to do, what to believe, and what others consider important. None of us is so secure that we don't need these kinds of anchors to fall back on from time to time.

Of course, you might want to clarify each concept. "Love thy neighbor." How? What is the most loving thing to do? To what extent are concepts or guidelines absolute? Such questions require that you examine yourself in the context of the concept. Holding yourself accountable for how you measure up to the concept means assuming responsibility for self—a tough challenge. Many people try to avoid it. Leaders, by virtue of the leadership responsibilities they have assumed, must not avoid accountability or self examination.

Third, psychological structure comes from *observing* patterns and processes. We learn from people and concepts, and we relate what we see and hear into patterns. As we become more skilled in observing our environment, we see how various pictures integrate into schemes and systems, which helps make sense of this complex world. We begin to understand that the world isn't just a disproportionate, random collection of unrelated elements, but, indeed, has an overall structure in which we are an integral part.

As we view ourselves in this vast system, it's our natural survival need to reduce our world to a manageable level. Geese in flight appear as a pattern or system, but each bird is, no doubt, more concerned about its own ability to keep up with the rest. So it is with people. We may be part of some grand, structured design, but our basic concern is self.

So, people perform their functions according to how they see the patterns from *their* perspective. All of us deal with our world from within our positions or roles. A mischievous little boy will see his world through young, inexperienced eyes. The punishing father will handle the world in a different way, as will the candidate for public office, the attorney, the physician, the leader.

Each of us functions from a number of different positions or roles every day. Most we take on with little conscious awareness. I can move from being a writer, a husband, a father, a supporter, a consultant, unaware of the shifts I am making in each role.

Problems arise when a person's roles conflict with what other people perceive a role should be. For example, a manager who sees himself as a kind, benevolent father—a role he enjoys at home—may transfer it to his work environment. However, his work group and his boss may see him as an authoritarian manager.

Or, a woman who sees herself as a concerned, doting mother will devote most of her energy to nurturing her children. When her children grow up, leave home, and begin relating to her as a friend, they will probably reject her continued attempts at the hovering mother role. Her primary role and her identity will be in tension.

The problem of conflicting roles can be lessened by looking beyond our roles and observing broader patterns. The manager can look beyond his fatherly role to the patterns of the workplace. The doting mother can observe the changes in her children. By observing these patterns, we get a new sense of our identity.

Discovering an organizing principle or pattern in our experience usually helps us feel positive and secure. When listening to a piece of music for the first time, I inevitably search for a unifying theme or melody that ties the piece together. When viewing an abstract painting, I appreciate it because of the artist's use of colors or its overall effect, but I also search for a theme or visual pattern that brings the work together.

Each of us needs and searches for structures that help us make sense of our surroundings. We derive structures from the three sources: physical, environmental and psychological. Our psychological structures come from people, concepts, and our ability to observe patterns in our experience. Those structures give us identity and support.

What Happens When Structure Decreases?

When structure decreases, discomfort results. A part of the discomfort is the surprise of losing something we need and have taken for granted. Water or air, for instance. Ever been on a hike and run out of water? I vividly recall hiking in a canyon expecting to refill my rapidly depleting canteen from a stream only to find it was a dusty wash. Anyone who has experienced a tornado knows the trauma of an air vacuum.

We surround ourselves with external structures that tell us who we are. When they are removed or diminished, the loss can have a devastating effect.

Here's an example: *Years ago, while serving in a psychological warfare unit during the Korean Conflict, my unit repatriated U.S. prisoners of war. The debriefing interviews we conducted revealed a great deal about the effects of sensory deprivation which, as you know, removes external structures. Many prisoners had been isolated in small cells, with little or no contact with the outside world. They told of developing elaborate games, such as tracing their lives historically or chronologically from their earliest memories. They designed incredible internal structures to compensate for the absence of a supportive external structure. Survival was, to a great degree, a matter of building upon their recollections and contriving intricate fantasies of their futures after release.*

Many people resist new situations because they fear the new will challenge their identity and change them. The fact is, it will! As you learn new ways of doing things, you change the way you see yourself. Acceptance of the new always challenges your identity and thus decreases the structure you have built up to protect your self.

Prejudice may result from self-protection. One of the most difficult pieces of new information to accept is new knowledge about people. As we learn about others, we inevitably learn about ourselves, which may be painful. One way of avoiding painful self-information is to avoid those who invoke it. The barriers of prejudice categorize groups of people. Bigots may make statements like "All blacks are lazy," or "You never saw a woman who could think like a man," and thus rule blacks and women out of their world. However, they have erected a defective structure since it denies reality and needs constant counterfeit reinforcement from like-minded bigots.

Another way people protect self-structure from new information is by reaffirming familiar roles. They resort to various strategies to lessen their discomfort. One strategy, well-known to training directors, is excessive use of cell phones. Participants in some training sessions often deal with new information about the way they view self and others. The most distressed get their employees back at the office to call them. The call reaffirms their identity by saying, in effect, "You are the boss and have special knowledge. We have a problem and only you can handle it." Having role and identity reaffirmed makes the participant secure enough to reenter the training session.

Physicians may use a similar strategy by having hospital staff or patients call them during a social engagement. A mother may do the same by having children call her at her husband's business party.

We protect ourselves in many different ways because the loss of structure is a painful experience. It often leads to depression. With the safe, dependable guidelines and predictable patterns of psychological sustenance gone or temporarily unavailable, the alarm called "anxiety" goes off. This "wake-up" call alerts us to the need for positive responsive action.

Fight/Flight Responses to Loss of Structure

There are two basic response patterns to a loss of structure—fight and flight. We seek structure because we need it. We find the absence of structure unpleasant and uncomfortable. We respond to the resulting stress in predictable ways.

The fight/flight response pattern ranges from healthy to maladaptive, from normal reactions to mental illness. Take a look at the figure on the next page.

Let's use a workplace promotion as an example and take a fight response first. One way of responding to stress caused by a lack of familiar structure is to work harder. If you were working eight hours a day, you begin working 10 hours. Nothing wrong with that for several weeks. Excessive hours over a long period of time, however, may indicate that you are using work as a way to avoid dealing with the stress of a promotion, which requires you to see yourself in a different way.

Another way to fight the unfamiliar is to argue. Small things set you off. You send critical memos. Or you deflect the stress onto those close to you—spouse, children, colleagues.

As your behavior moves toward maladaptive, you begin to complain more. Nothing seems to go right for you and you find fault with your subordinates continuously. This behavior is often followed by a verbal fight and a belligerent chip-on-the-shoulder approach to people.

Next, you become so distressed you cause those around you to have accidents. The distress you feel becomes so acute that it's contagious.

Finally, you may physically attack someone. Battered spouses and children are often the victims. This response signals illness; the attacking person needs professional help.

The second basic response to stress is flight. Still using the example of a recent promotion, one healthy way to flee or withdraw is to

NORMAL ———————————————► ILLNESS

FIGHT						
Work	Excessive Work	Arguments Angry memos Anger deflected onto wife or children	Excessive complaints	Constantly fighting Belligerent attitude	Causing accidents	Physical attack
FLIGHT						
Sleep	Sleeping all weekend or watching television throughout weekend	Withdrawal Not hearing wife or children	Avoid work Doing less and accomplishing less. Spending time in other interests.	Quits trying and plateaus out	Having accidents	Physical immobility

Figure 1. Response to a Promotion (an example of what happens when structure decreases)

sleep a few extra hours at night or take an occasional weekend nap, or increase TV watching or computer game playing time. Nothing wrong with this. It becomes maladaptive when the withdrawal becomes excessive. Sleeping all weekend, or retreating to the den to watch every sports event that ESPN can schedule over the weekend is a clear indication of not wanting to be involved with family or friends.

As flight or withdrawal increases, you don't listen to family members. Further, you start going into the office later and take longer lunch breaks. You find reasons to be out of town or to miss meetings. Even more maladaptive, you begin to plateau out in your job. Your ambition, energy and drive decrease. You avoid new responsibilities, become resigned to the current job, and do just enough work not to lose it.

You may have a convenient accident to get out of current responsibilities or, even more common, become conveniently sick—something you learned how to do before the age of four. When you're sick, people tend not to hold you responsible; they feel sorry for you and want to take care of you.

And finally, on this possible continuum, you become physically immobilized. Your physician can't find anything physically wrong with you, but you somehow can't get out of bed. You have reached the level of illness where professional help is a necessity if you are to recover.

During fight or flight responses, people justify their actions with numerous reasons why they do what they do. In both patterns, they're exhibiting distress and they believe no one else can appreciate or understand what they're going through.

The earlier on in this continuum a person or his superiors or colleagues can recognize the signs of distress and take action, the better chance of resolving the situation.

Thoughts on Leadership

Leaders, be aware there is a high correlation between incompetence and laziness.

Be wary of folks who exhibit no passion for life. They may be indifferent toward the conditions that surround their lives or so rigidly controlled that their emotions have atrophied. Or, they may fear that exposure of emotions undermines their self-image. In any event, they are unlikely to make much of a contribution to whatever project you are pursuing.

What these people haven't learned is that living life on the surface courts nothingness. Participating in life to the depth of your being is where you find excitement, passion, and joy. There is little chance of experiencing life's fullness if you do not explore the rich resources that exist within.

Every leader should know that competence and expertise are important characteristics to develop, but the primary indication of a leader's worth is significance. What positive difference are you making in the lives of others?

Learn to prioritize and your life-management problems will be considerably reduced.

The leader who wills her beliefs and judgment to another is mortally weakened.

Don't Go There, Leaders

What admirable creatures we humans are!

Place us in challenging situations and we have this remarkable ability to perform mighty acts. We look romantically at the moon for ages, then decide it's worth visiting. Which we do!

What would it be like to send messages instantly around the world? We can do that! Create new forms of life? Done! And when we witness suffering in the world, we respond with a generosity that astonishes.

Identify a seemingly insolvable problem and we see the opportunities to overcome it. An exciting species, we are!

Which is why our continued engagement in human pettiness diminishes us in such profound ways.

It's as if the human spirit, incalculably noble in times of huge challenges, crisis and human suffering, feels the need to soil itself when interacting with people on a daily basis.

We work with colleagues and friends in our organizations who do praiseworthy acts while balancing family and jobs, often in miraculous ways, yet we complain about their "stupidity" and their glaring imperfections. We are obstinately capable of overlooking our own flaws, yet energetically able to identify and articulate defects of others.

Somehow we fail to understand that in diminishing the qualities of others, we diminish ourselves even more. In concentrating on the negative characteristics outside of our control, we consign ourselves to be less than we can be.

I am reminded of the admonition attributed to Jesus, "Why do you look at the speck of sawdust in your brother's eye and pay no attention to the plank in your own eye?"

There is something each of us can do about this human failing. We can spend more time with ourselves, contemplating our own flaws and how to overcome them. Including why we feel the need to denigrate others.

In reflective moments when we can be honest with ourselves, it's possible for an exalted self-image to give way to a realistic self-portrait. It's in moments of clarity that we acknowledge our self-centeredness and our proclivity to project onto others our own deficiencies.

I believe strongly that leaders can be major influences in this regard. People need role models from whom they can learn and emulate. Leaders teach by who they are, by what they say, and by how they treat others. Relating to people in caring ways while voicing and communicating encouraging, positive messages is bound to have a salutary affect on followers. Likewise, criticism of others tends to encourage similar pettiness in followers—it endorses negativity as followers assume that "if our leader does it, it must be all right."

It's important that leaders recognize their own limitations and help others understand that imperfections are human and that we bear responsibility for coping with our own. At the same time, it's important for leaders to help followers become aware that we do not have the power to make situations or others perfect.

One of life's great challenges is to transcend one's own inevitable flaws while building relationships with others that transcend theirs as well.

Pettiness empties the human spirit, imprisons love, and reduces reciprocal opportunities for personal growth and renewal.

In other words, leaders, it's not worth it!

So, don't go there!

And be the kind of leader who discourages others from going there as well.

Taking Humor Seriously

Konrad Lorenz said it: "Humor and knowledge are the two great hopes of civilization."

I'm impressed he suggested the two components in that order.

It seems to me most leaders don't take humor seriously enough.

Granted, there are reasons for this oversight. Throughout history, political leaders have been portrayed as individuals who took themselves too seriously. Read the great philosophers and you may rightly conclude they were humorless individuals. Check out the writings of seminal theologians; they, too, looked at the world with a scowling countenance. Exceptions are few.

These three historical, highly influential sources shaped the world in which we live. Humorous is not an adjective one would use to describe the enormous contributions they made to society.

While reading the body of literature they left behind may give us a perspective on the major forces of humankind's development, it leaves us poorly equipped to appreciate the unending comedies that punctuate history.

So, for historical balance, if not accuracy, we should never underestimate the serious contributions made by the irreverent men and women who have stood near the world's leaders and poked fun at their shenanigans.

Molière, Shakespeare, Dickens, Twain, Parker, Rogers, Sahl, Grizzard, and Hope are just a few who have ably served society by pricking the balloons of pomposity and self-righteousness.

It is difficult to remain sanctimonious when quipsters are in the vicinity. In fact, it's downright dangerous! A leader with a tendency toward self-deceiving arrogance or pretentiousness is a prime candidate for chastisement and derision. Political cartoonists and certain columnists thrive on such behavior.

Perhaps, due largely to the piercing wit of today's humorists, there is acceptance of the idea that a person lacking self-effacing humor may be unqualified to lead others. We tend to be put off, if not turned fully away, by those who exhibit a deficiency in this regard.

Which is why humor must be taken more seriously. It is, perhaps, the best antidote to preventing leaders from forming delusions of self-importance and fostering the destructive kind of self-deceit that elevates personal pride above true servanthood.

Of course, most leaders do not serve on the national stage, so they don't draw the attention of an Ivins or a Barry. Consequently, they should "go it on their own" and develop a sense of self that sees the humor in their actions, observes their behavior with a skeptical smile, and looks at the world with a whimsical approach.

Effective leaders understand that their basic humanity is best served by nurturing a balance in their lives that includes making room for humor and comedy.

Thoughts on Leadership

A person's character may be defined by the distance between speech and actions. How often do we hear people rant, rave, and criticize, yet do nothing about a situation? If using strong words, their actions should involve risk. Otherwise, they may be rightly called cowards. Cowardice is anathema to the effective leader.

Moral cowardice is found both in indifference toward suffering and in the failure to act on behalf of others in times of crisis. Ignoring the clear needs of people is a reprehensible act.

Leaders, know your limitations and weaknesses; there are some folks with malice in their hearts who will aim for them every time.

Leaders, know your tender spots. Then determine whether to protect or expose them, and to whom. You will be happier if they are not subject to surprise.

Commend, leaders, commend! Think what your friends and followers mean to you, then make a practice of commending those who, day after day, behave and work in ways that reflect credit on you as well as themselves.

Learn to think critically and you decrease the chances of falling for the superficial or being taken in by deceitful individuals.

The Value of Ignorance

I want to say a few kind words about ignorance.

It's been getting a bad rap, as if there's something wrong with being ignorant.

For some odd reason, it hasn't registered with people that everyone—including leaders—begins life ignorant. It's through experiences and choices that we gain knowledge in a relatively few areas. In the early years, our need to survive directs the lessons. Increasingly, as we mature, we augment these learnings by making critical choices that shape our lives.

But no matter how much we learn, or how dedicated we are to learning, we're all ignorant in some areas about some things. I'm a technological ignoramus. In numerous fields—geology, mathematics, physics, chemistry, botany, aeronautics, auto mechanics, horse breeding, farming, medicine, to name just a few—my knowledge is in a low percentile.

However, there's another kind of ignorance that concerns me about leaders. It's believing you know more than you do. Bertrand Russell put it this way: "The trouble with the world today is that the stupid are cocksure, while the intelligent are full of doubts."

Recently, I listened to a cocksure leader in love with his opinions. He was certain of what most of his listeners regarded as questionable "facts." He said nothing with the slightest degree of hesitation or qualification. He couldn't imagine how any of us could disagree with his pronouncements.

Personally, I admire Sacha Gultrey's point of view: "The little I know, I owe to my ignorance."

In my experience, the earlier a person latches on to certainties, the more doubts that person is likely to have in later life. I believe confusion is a given when one is young, or even middle-aged, for that matter. In fact, if you're not confused, I suspect you aren't thinking clearly or have developed some serious biases and prejudices you are likely to regret in the later years. At least, I hope this kind of person will.

Like ignorance, confusion is not necessarily a negative. To be confused is to have doubts, and as Tennyson wrote, "There lives more faith in honest doubt, believe me, than in half the creeds."

So, let's not be too harshly critical of ignorance. It has an honorable history, at least in my life, and I suspect in yours as well.

The trick is to keep learning, leaders, about leadership issues, skills, and principles while never acting as if you know more than you do.

I-Thou Relationships

"He called me a what?"

"She really said those things?"

Most of us—if not all of us—have had the experience of being called names. We've likely responded in the above manner.

Leaders, who often put themselves out front of the crowd, are fair game for derogatory comments. Not to expect them is naive.

What leaders learn, of course, is that there is a lack of civility throughout the land. And folks who stick their necks out are likely targets.

It's tempting when attacked by critics who make their attacks personal and vindictive, to want to strike back in a like manner. It's human nature to want to do so. But, that lowers one to the level of the critic and, frankly, casts a shadow on your leadership qualifications. No matter how unfair and vitriolic the attack, a leader needs to stay above that kind of negative, hurtful exchange.

I'd like to suggest that leaders would do well to prepare themselves for this probable unpleasant experience by reading a book titled *I and Thou*, written some years ago by the Jewish theologian, Martin Buber. If you've already read it, I suspect you'll agree with me that it's one of the most important and revolutionary books of the past century.

Buber tells us that the most mature kind of relationship between two people is the I-Thou relationship. It exists when two people recognize each other's differences but form a bond based on love.

Most relationships are not in this category. More common is the I-You relationship, which recognizes the basic humanity of each other, but neither loves the other. Each person does, however, value and respect the other person.

Buber describes another relationship and in this one, he exposes us to a key issue in human interactions and society. He calls it the I-It relationship. It exists when a person sees another as a subhuman, or even inanimate object; an "It" to be used as we would a hammer or a footstool.

Being human, we have a tendency to label those who attack us as "Its." It's satisfying to write them off as such, but we don't ennoble ourselves by doing so. Perhaps we can't bring ourselves to even think about the I-Thou category; maybe the best we can do is shoot for the I-You approach.

But what we should try to understand is that Buber's major point is that every one of us—all human beings, regardless of race, religious faith, sexual orientation, and ethnicity—is a precious individual.

Incivility has its roots in I-It relationships as it does in bigotry. An effective leader simply can't stoop so low as to wallow in that kind of relationship. We expect better of our leaders.

And leaders need to expect better of themselves.

Buber's perspective is worth reading about and internalizing insofar as it is possible.

Thoughts on Leadership

One of the great tragedies of the human condition is that we prefer to act in ways we already know, even when evidence shows these ways are inefficient and ineffective, than to try new approaches that have a possibility of creating better conditions and improving our lives.

Please, if elected to office, serve the public, not yourself. When a community, state or our nation's elected leadership is paralyzed by fear of losing the next election, then a reactive approach to issues and problems elevates personal concerns to a priority that subjects the common good to secondary status. Those who seek the illusion of personal power contribute to the reality of political impotence.

Seeking to improve yourself doesn't necessarily mean—for leaders especially—improving your circumstances.

Leaders, cultivate creativity. And remember that an imaginative mind has disorderly components. In other words, you'll "never get it all together!" So, don't worry about it!

Emulation honors the recipient, imitation flatters. The person who follows another's lead retains her own identity; the imitator risks losing hers.

Complacency and Indifference

I have a problem with the words complacency and indifference.

I hope every leader has the same problem!

I may be in the minority here, but that doesn't dissuade me from wishing that more folks harbored the same attitude. Or, from hoping that young people gain an abhorrence of those words.

You see, I want youngsters to become imbued with the spirit of discontent. I want them to be dissatisfied with who they are, what they're learning, the way we are treating our environment, and the condition of the world. I want them to understand that progress is made by those who do not accept things as they are.

It's a tough lesson to learn, but the young need to know that only people who are dissatisfied with the world around them move forward. Those who are content with their lives either stand still, fall behind, or get in the way of those who are trying to improve the human condition.

I want to see people frustrated with the way society treats the homeless, upset with the epidemic drug problem, and commit themselves to devote at least part of their time and energies to work for a more humane and just society. Complacent people don't get angry about these kind of problems. In fact, they prefer not to know about them at all.

Nor, of course, do people who are indifferent toward others, who lack a concern or interest in the lives of others. Whether because of a self-centered attitude, lack of compassion, or because they have insulated their lives from human suffering, their indifference reflects an impoverished soul.

To have a reverence toward life, one can ill afford to permit the spirit within to wither and atrophy. The human spirit courts adventure just as it seeks freedom. A personal vision of a better world nurtures the spirit while a complacent spirit arrests its development. A person's spirit is damaged by an uncaring attitude toward the evils inflicted on one's brothers and sisters wherever they live. While human tragedy is universal, it need not be an accepted fact of life. It can, at least, be ameliorated if enough people care and commit themselves to changing the conditions that foster human suffering.

I want young people to grow up accustomed to the swirling currents of change, prepared and eager to humanize the future. Only if they accept change as a constant and are determined to be agents of humane change will they have a chance of realizing their potentials as people who will leave the world a better place than they found it.

They will have little chance, of course, unless the previous generations provide leadership to show them the way. And none of us will be responsible leaders or role models until we pledge ourselves to actively fight the twin peaks of complacency and indifference.

Years ago, the author James Baldwin, in an extemporaneous speech to New York City public school teachers, put the challenge this way: "The young may not listen to us, but they never fail to imitate us, for indeed, what other models do they have?"

Thoughts on Leadership

Honest dedication to self-awareness is a major key to healthy, positive relationships. Lack of insight into self and the "whys" of behavior, attitudes and beliefs is a primary reason for communication failures between people.

Behavior that includes posturing and posing will not be trusted or respected. The posturing public self disqualifies the private self from living with integrity. The necessity of acting out different roles produces an inconsistency that undermines a leader's ability to lead.

If a leader wishes to appeal to a wide cross-section of citizens as opposed to those with narrow agendas, she must clearly identify the line that separates commitment from zealotry.

An effective leader understands that while it is good to excel in areas of competence, it is wise to be ordinary in exhibiting them. The less one advertises abilities and skills, the more he will be esteemed.

Leaders, be wary of folks who persist in telling you they must learn to say "no" to requests on their time. This response often masks a need to be asked. Their egos frequently require your recognition that they are busy and desperately needed by others. Either that or they have not learned the skill of setting priorities.

Leaders and the Morale Curve

When I was conducting seminars around the country in the 1970s and 80s, I introduced leaders to the morale curve. Most of the time, I was invited to talk about change, of which the morale curve was one part. During and after the seminar, it was the curve that elicited most of the questions and about which seminar participants talked with the most excitement, as they related personal stories.

For most people, exposure to the morale curve is a genuine eye-opener—one of those profound "ah-ha" experiences.

So, let's take a look at it.

It was over thirty years ago while working at The Menninger Foundation that I became fascinated with this particular psychological principle. What grabbed my attention was how uncannily it described my behavior and explained what I had been going through. I have continued to study it and now believe it is the single most significant psychological principle I have ever come across.

Not only does the morale curve explain a great deal about morale, it also beams a bright light on how structure and support are affected by change.

Study Figure 2 on the next page for a moment:

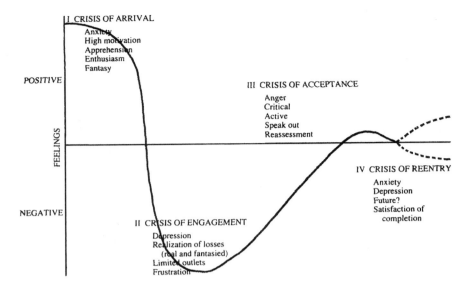

Figure 2. The Morale Curve

The curve illustrates the ups and downs of personal morale a person experiences when making a role change of any kind; e.g., new job, new baby, new task, new relationship, new home, new assignment. It reflects the underlying psychological processes that occur when people lose the supportive structure they are accustomed to.

Peace Corps volunteers experienced such loss. In the early years of the Peace Corps in the 1960s, Dr. Walter Menninger and others were asked to look for reasons why so many volunteers resigned before their two-year tour was completed. In the course of his extensive interviews and examination of related data, Dr. Menninger discovered problems of behavior that he later reduced to a formula: the morale curve. Using the morale curve, he was able to identify the flow of feelings the volunteers experienced as they moved through their tour of duty.

The initial stage on the curve he called the *crisis of arrival*. The word "crisis" is used to connote a point of crucial focus and does not signify the negative implication we usually attach to it. Volunteers had very positive feelings upon entering a new country. While they were anxious and apprehensive at facing unknowns, they were highly motivated to do a good job, and enthusiastic about the opportunity to make a contribution to the native people and to save the world (fantasy).

Several months after beginning work, morale and motivation decreased, hitting bottom between the fourth and seventh month. Volunteers reached the second stage of the curve, the *crisis of engagement*. They discovered the assignment was not what they expected and began to experience significant losses as a result of having left their mother country. The support the volunteers had taken for granted from friends, parents, and family was mostly gone. The old, familiar structures they had unconsciously counted on were no longer available.

In addition, they were forced to acknowledge that many of their fantasies (saving the world, living an exciting life, gratitude from people, admired as heroes) would have to be abandoned. The realization of these losses triggered feelings of profound frustration that resulted in a real dilemma because of their limited outlets for expression. One usually responds to frustration with anger. However, it was difficult for Peace Corps volunteers to ventilate their anger for two reasons. First, the old familiar outlets were unavailable—friends, family, sports. Second, they didn't want to offend the people they had so recently befriended and with whom they were trying to work closely to accomplish agreed-upon tasks.

With the customary ways of expressing anger denied, they became depressed. Their anger turned inward. Not having had previous experience with these kinds of frustrations, coupled with the deadening blow of losing their fantasies, was more than many of the volunteers could take. They were the ones who resigned and returned home.

Those who remained and somehow coped with the frustration and loss, moved into the third phase, the *crisis of acceptance.* By then, they had worked within their community, become more comfortable in their surroundings, set new structures for their lives, and were receiving support from coworkers and new friends. Feeling more comfortable, they became critical of the Peace Corps for failing to prepare them for their present realities. As the volunteers criticized, they reassessed their situation. They took more control of their lives. Expression of anger and frustration relieved depression. Released from depression, they had more energy for constructive work. The more active they became, the higher their morale elevated or advanced. They questioned themselves and the Corps as they relinquished old ideas and formed new priorities.

The volunteers had one more crisis to face—the *crisis of reentry,* which the volunteers met with mixed feelings. Their two-year tour completed, they felt satisfaction with their work but recognized it was time to say goodbye. They had to face losses again. The support system they had built and the structures they had developed would be torn asunder. The thought brought on depression. They were anxious about how their home and friends had changed during their absence, and how they would be accepted since they, too, had changed. Some returned with moderately positive morale and some were mildly depressed, depending on how and whether they worked through the anger and depression provoked by their new losses. None, however, returned at as high a morale level as when they entered their Corps assignment. The reason? No one can sustain fantasy.

Since life is a succession of role and identity changes, the curve occurs frequently. Each of us is in a number of roles simultaneously (friend, spouse, son or daughter, parent, employee, supervisor, leader, student). Each role is somewhere on the morale curve.

Think of examples from your life. Did you ever get married? Did you enter at the top? I did! But it didn't take us many months to begin discussions like:

"Are you going to put those things in your hair every night when you go to bed?" (Can you imagine her saying that to me?)

"Are you going to hang your clothes on the carpet every time you change?"

"Do you realize the toothpaste tube will also squeeze from the bottom up?"

"Stool seats that go up can also be put back down!"

Has anyone had a marriage that started high and remained there? I doubt it. The ones I know about are much like mine—a roller coaster with many ups and downs.

The curve is easily identified with incoming college freshmen. The *crisis of engagement* (commonly called the pits!) hits between Thanksgiving and Christmas. At Christmas vacation, students compare notes with former high school classmates and discover they haven't got it so bad: the *crisis of acceptance*. Morale goes back up until the end of the first year: *crisis of reentry*. The freshmen leave their first year with slightly negative or slightly positive feelings.

A job change or promotion is another example, with the bottom of the curve being reached somewhere between the fourth and seventh month.

Leaders, every time you assume a new leadership position of responsibility, you'll go through the curve. Check it out!

The morale curve describes the process we go through each time our role is changed. It shows us the sequence we follow when we confront the losses of old supports and structures and develop new ones to restore equilibrium and a sense of identity.

Our goal is that idealistic and, thus, unattainable state of homeostasis: the self in perfect balance with the environment. We never achieve it because our physical, environmental, and psychological structures change continually.

Can a person avoid going through the curve? This is a fair and reasonable question since most people (masochists excluded) do not enjoy being depressed. The answer is yes, but consider the consequences. The straight line in the middle of the diagram in Figure 2 is the line of indifference or neutrality: no positive feelings, no negative feelings. An example would be the person up for promotion who says to his supervisor, "I don't care what you do with me. I don't have any feelings about it. Do what you want." Is that person likely to receive the promotion? No. The supervisor wants to see the *crisis of arrival* characteristics: high motivation, enthusiasm, and apprehension.

If you invest yourself in your roles (if you care!) you *will* go through the curve. If you try to avoid the curve, you'll probably stop getting promotions or having much fun in your life. The closer you move toward indifference, the fewer the thrills, the less excitement.

This brings us to an important formula. In human behavior there are few formulas you can count on. Here is one.

Change is the one constant in life; it occurs in many variations daily. As I explained in the section, "Leaders and Change," one way or another, change always involves loss. Loss results initially in frustration, and frustration produces anger. There are two ways to handle anger: either you get it out, or it goes inside of you. The latter is the genesis of depression.

The lesson is clear. When depressed, get busy. Then discover the source of your anger. Express it constructively. It's not the time to go on vacation. The worst thing to do when depressed is nothing. Ask for help from family, friends or therapists if you're having trouble pulling out of the pits. Keep in mind that everyone is depressed from time to time. It's no big deal to be depressed for several days. However, if you're depressed for several weeks or months, you probably need help.

Another issue about the pits or the *crisis of engagement* merits attention. Most resignations occur when a person is at the bottom of the curve. That's when people quit jobs, marriages, school, or the Peace Corps. Few resignations occur when a person is in the positive feeling zone.

The bottom of the curve is also when suicides occur, especially when the major roles in your life—spouse, parent, job, for instance—have bottomed out.

The pits is no time to make major life or job decisions. Work your way out of depression, then see how the situation looks.

If you are a supervisor or manager, be sensitive to the curve so you can help employees who are in the *crisis of engagement*. Two approaches you may use: talk them through their depression to help them get their anger out, or assign them extra work. The latter strategy may make them mad as hell at you, but they're unlikely to remain depressed. (By the way, more work may be accomplished during the *crisis of acceptance* than during any of the other phases; anger is a powerful stimulant!) Leaders, do not let employees resign or transfer to another division when they're in the pits if you can help it. It's not necessary to lose a valuable employee you have spent time and money training.

If employees resign at the low point of the morale curve, they are likely to do the same thing the next time they hit the *crisis of engagement.* Job hoppers rarely survive the pits. When things get tough, they bail out. The same pattern can be observed in the various roles people take on—spouses divorcing, students leaving school, leaders quitting groups.

The real challenge is to stay in the role. To do so, each of us needs structure and support.

Structure, Support and the Morale Curve— An Illustration

Let's examine the morale curve as it relates to structure and support. Here is an illustration that should provide leaders with information and insights into how they can be of assistance to others experiencing the morale curve.

Imagine a man who pulls up roots and leaves friends, community, and job to accept a position in another company, community, and state.

In all probability the decision is not easy, perhaps involving difficult family decisions, but the man is excited by the new challenges and the increased psychological and material benefits. He voluntarily gives up supportive and meaningful structures, believing the rewards of change outweigh the losses.

One loss he may not recognize: with those supportive roots that provided a sense of identity go most of his defenses. He becomes more vulnerable.

The first psychological task he faces in the *crisis of arrival* is coping with fear of the unknown. Many, if not most, of the comfortable, supportive constructs that bound his life are gone. The familiar "knowns" that gave his life a meaningful context in which to work are no longer available. In their places are a series of unknowns within which he must build a new work life and identity. It's no easy job.

Often overlooked is the even more stressful situation the rest of the family faces. The man has the organizational support system and structures to move into. His wife and children must discover their own resources.

During the *crisis of arrival*, he gets into the job as soon as possible. Becoming involved diminishes his anxiety of the unknown while enabling him to begin setting new structures that will soon provide support.

However, his supervisor is a part of the unknown fears which, however unrealistic, are quite real to a new employee. The supervisor may be able to counteract the man's fears by providing a clear structure: specific goals, priorities, standards, objectives. If the supervisor encourages the new employee to use trusted ways of handling problems that worked for him in the old job, his fears will diminish.

As job involvement increases, the employee builds the supports and structures that restore his identity, albeit with some necessary modifications to the new surroundings. He is now ready to deal with the psychological issues of the *crisis of engagement*—loss, frustration, and depression.

After several months of involvement in routine work tasks, the enthusiasm and excitement wane and he recognizes that his fantasies will not be realized. He realizes he is working with some real turkeys—a few even worse than those he left.

There is another aspect of the fantasy problem. Just as he had fantasized that he wouldn't have to work with losers any more, so his new group had unrealistic fantasies about him. Their disappointment comes at the time he most needs their support.

He also becomes aware of losses he had heretofore overlooked during the excitement of the move. It all adds up. Not understanding what's happening can be frustrating and cause depression, unless, of course, he gets his feelings out in a controlled, positive manner.

This is the time for his supervisor to help him and the group deal with their anger through discussion and/or hard work. But most important, the man must begin to accept his new role, to deal with the organization and his group in realistic ways. He must give up the unrealistic fantasies that prevent him from seeing himself and the organization clearly and objectively.

As the man comes to grip with the anger provoked by his losses, he reaches the *crisis of acceptance*. The problem is how to appropriately express the anger. Telling others, "I'm angry because I lost my fantasies" goes over like the proverbial lead balloon. Further, his conscience usually asks, "What right do I have to be angry?"

However, as the man continues to involve himself in his job tasks with success, the opportunities to express his anger arise. He feels he can be critical. Once he has a sense of accomplishment from tackling tough issues successfully, he feels qualified to express some degree of anger.

Most often he channels anger as constructive criticism. If he receives support or acceptance for speaking out, he will likely enter into a benevolent cycle rather than a malicious cycle. As he criticizes, which releases his anger, he frees up energy for constructive work. The more constructive work he accomplishes, the more he feels justified to criticize. The more he criticizes, the more anger he discharges. The criticism becomes less frequent. The anger dissolves.

He reassesses his new role in the organization, which means he reexamines his identity. With this reevaluation, he becomes more actively involved in the organization, which improves his morale and motivation. By then he has established a fairly effective support system and set the necessary structures that enable him to perform comfortably and effectively. The probability of his becoming a long-term employee increases.

It's no coincidence that people who stay more than a year in an organization tend to remain.

The man's supervisor can be helpful during the *crisis of acceptance* by understanding that it is a true crisis. If he reflects on his past, he can recall his own experiences in the curve. Recognizing the crisis as legitimate, he accepts critical statements as a natural and normal expression of anger. He need not take the comments personally.

However, the supervisor should set a structure that keeps the anger appropriate and in bounds. Anger expressed inappropriately— fighting, sabotaging others' efforts, name-calling, taking drugs, heavy drinking—should not be tolerated.

The supervisor can support the new employee by increased use of the man's talents, by encouraging him to talk through his anger, and by helping him reassess his role in the organization. By listening to him in an understanding yet realistic way, the supervisor helps the new employee feel more a part of the new situation.

The fourth stage, the *crisis of reentry,* is not part of the morale curve in this illustration. The reentry process occurs only when the identity or role change is time-limited. As the Peace Corps demonstrated, a person in such cases unconsciously prepares to deal with the role change while feeling the losses of leaving a present situation. While both anxious and eager to start a new challenge, persons in a time-limited change must deal with the losses of support and structure only recently developed. Whether they leave the present position with high or low morale depends on whether they work through the depression brought on by these losses.

How To Build Structure Into Your Life

To begin, leaders, use the morale curve as a forecast for change, and plan accordingly. I believe the morale curve is one of the few patterns you can, with reasonable assurance, *forecast*. When a person makes a role change, a predictable sequence follows.

Do keep in mind that it is easier to see others in the curve than yourself. At this moment, you are in a number of curves. Why don't you take some time now to see if you can identify where you are on the curves in several of your major roles—spouse, son or daughter, father or mother, employee or employer, leader.

Also, be aware that each curve you are in impacts on every other curve. A job role change affects your identity as a spouse or parent, just as a role change in your family affects your work role. Your identity is made up of many roles, each of which contributes to solidifying or fragmenting your sense of identity. Since your roles are always changing, your identity is always changing. Who you are today is different than who you were five, ten, twenty years ago. Your changing roles keep your identity in motion.

The above is true if you are *involved* in your different roles. Remember, the middle line on the curve is the line of indifference. No positive feelings, no negative feelings. Those who try to avoid the curve and live a life of indifference or apathy have likely been badly wounded. They have been painfully hurt by their losses and have decided to spend their lives guarding against involvement. They are so sensitive to the loss coming up at the end of a relationship or situation that they refuse any involvement. In this manner, they don't lose anything when they leave. They may well avoid the feelings of anger and depression, but they also miss out on the warm, loving feelings that develop in relationships. Entering a relationship empty-handed ensures leaving the same way.

A striking and all-too-common example is a lousy marriage and bitter divorce. Soon after the split, it's not unusual to hear statements like, "Whew, never again. I'm never going to get married again!" The person doesn't want the pain of that level of involvement. The loss produced more suffering than any potential gain in the future. However, after several months, and often several years, the individual discovers that indifference is worse. If you are indifferent to others, indifference from others is what you tend to receive. And if you give love, you tend to receive love in return.

Most of us opt for love, even though we know that when we give it, we're going "to get it," one way or another.

A second pattern of behavior for a person who has survived a rotten marriage is to try to enter the next marriage somewhere between positive feelings (high on the curve) and the line of indifference. In effect, the person says to the new mate, "I'm only going to give you so much love because the last time I got too involved I got hurt. So this time I'm going to hold back on my commitment."

Is this fair? Of course not! To neither of them. Any relationship involves pain as well as joy. No relationship is alive if marked by indifference or a lack of reciprocal commitment.

Another way to avoid the curve is to enter a new role below the indifference line, with negative feelings. This occurs when a person makes an unwanted role change, such as a job demotion or transfer to an undesirable city, an unwanted pregnancy, getting drafted into a war one opposes, or being forced into a marriage.

During the course of a person's life, the *curves will balance out* most of the time. When you are below the middle line in the negative zone at work, you may be in the positive zone at home. The reverse can also be true. Since a person is constantly in a number of different roles, each of which is changing, the law of probability is that most curves will balance out through the years.

However, since each curve affects every other curve, a major role or identity change—such as the death of a spouse or child, or the loss of a job—can alter the other curves dramatically. A major loss can drag the other curves down. The chances of a severe depression increase. In a number of suicides I have observed, the victims had a high incidence of multiple curves in the negative zone. The world looks dark when the major roles in your life are all at the bottom of the curve.

In handling the many curves a person is going through, the ability to adapt is paramount. The more adaptable you are, the better you will cope with the negative aspects of the curve.

The morale curve explains much about our response to change and our dependence upon structure. The loss of structure sends morale plummeting. And while there, the degree of support we experience is a major determinant of how long we remain depressed.

The curve is a clear behavioral example of the direct effect of structure and support. The more you observe the curve in your own life and the lives of those with whom you work, live, and lead, the better will you appreciate its significance.

Here are some further guidelines and suggestions to use in assessing the structures that bind your life and the support systems that help you cope with the inevitable problems and stresses you face daily. Taking these guidelines and suggestions to heart should help you deal constructively with the morale curve.

Need

First, leaders, recognize your legitimate need for structure. It's just as real as the air you breathe and the water you drink. When your air supply is cut off, you feel an immediate panic. When your source of water suddenly stops, the loss may not produce sudden fear, but you feel the same kind of anxiety in time.

Examine your physical, environmental, and psychological sources of structure. Take a sheet of paper and divide it into three columns. In the first column, list the physical structures that give you support. In the second column, list environmental structures, and in the third, psychological. Are they adequate? If not, work to shore up those parts that are lacking.

On another sheet of paper, write an action plan. Plan one simple action a week to improve your personal structures.

Identity

Strive to be psychologically healthy by not losing your self in your roles. Because of the commitments and responsibilities leaders tend to take on, you cannot afford to confuse your roles with your identity. Lose your self and you'll have only your roles left.

Peter Sellers was one of the great actors of his time. Upon his death, one of his children remarked on how well he played his roles but that he never knew himself. As a person he was lost; only as an actor was he sure of himself.

I've witnessed far too many people experience an organizational death when they retire. With the cessation of their organizational roles they appeared to have little reason to live. They had put their energy into developing a role and had none left to nurture the self. A large number of them became easy prey for the numerous illnesses that can plague people in their retirement years.

Here's an exercise to help separate your roles from your self. On 3-inch by 5-inch cards, list every role you play in your life. Write one role on each card. When you have finished identifying your roles, arrange the cards in order of their priority to you. Select the most important role and put it on top. Place the second most important role next, and so forth until you have the least important role on the bottom.

Turn the stack of cards face down, so the least important role is on top. Pick that card up and think about that role for a minute. Put it aside, away from the other cards. Think about how you would feel without that role in your life.

Work your way through the stack of cards in the same manner. Think about each role, discard it, and think about how you would feel without it. Most folks find this task emotionally draining. It's hard work. Take it slow and easy. You need not complete the entire stack in one sitting.

When you've finished going through the cards, sit for a few minutes and think how it would be to have none of your current roles. You may find it upsetting; you may find it relieving. Let your feelings be whatever they are. Examine them. Let them give you information about your identity, who you are beyond your roles.

When you finish examining your feelings, select the roles you want to keep in your life. You may discover that some of the roles are not necessary or desirable. Get rid of them by putting those cards aside. Rearrange the remaining cards in order of their priority.

Roots

Develop your roots. What roots in your life provide the most support? Your spouse, parents, children, friends, church, God, organizations, self, work, knowledge?

Each of us has an extensive root system that enables us to stand steady against constant change. We must have solid roots that permit us to bend, but not to break; to lose some of our roles (limbs) at times, but not our self (trunk).

Nourish your roots and build strong ones so that when you lose one (death of a parent, job loss), you can call on the others for the necessary sustaining strength to go on with life. When a person has only a few roots, or shallow ones that are undernourished, losses are more devastatingly painful. Roots provide structure and support.

Time

Set guidelines for yourself so that you use your time to the best advantage. Managing time well provides a structure to your days that will reduce daily stresses—unless, of course, you become obsessive-compulsive about it. At that point, time controls you rather than the reverse.

Gain control over as much of your time as possible, or your life is going to be structured by others and by things. It's similar to riding a horse. If you're in charge, you set the pace and direction. If the beast is in charge, you have to hold on for dear life.

Change

Remember that we live in a world of rapid change. Familiar landmarks and guideposts seem to disappear daily. Diminished structure produces anxiety.

As the world accelerates, pick out a few things you treasure and hold on to them—music, plays, favorite organizations, books, mountain paths, sunsets, rain, friends.

You may not be able to stop the world and get off, but you can decelerate from time to time by slowing yourself down.

Balance

Work to achieve balance in your life—between change and stability, between personal and professional life, between family and work, between duty and freedom. Balance is the central organizing concept of all structures, and may well be the essential quality of our physical structure.

Freedom comes not from the absence of structure, but from appropriate structure, humanely applied. The overly structured person loses much richness in life; the unstructured person finds little. Seek balance. Structure and support follow in a nourishing, self-fulfilling, and personally rewarding way.

Thoughts on Leadership

In my experience, the most effective leaders possess considerable self-knowledge. They somehow understand that self-awareness is a window through which they can view realities. Those who lack this insight tend to view reality through a mirror—everything is distorted by their self-centered image.

Leaders, know your coping mechanisms! Denial, for instance, is a fascinating coping technique. The more pervasive the threat to our welfare, the more vigorous is our denial that we are threatened. Strangely, in the face of a frightening set of circumstances, we often retreat back into the behavior that caused the threat in the first place. Thus, we take precisely the wrong action at the wrong time, then wonder why our "tried and true" behavior doesn't work. It seems some of us would rather go down to defeat doing what we've always done, than meet a challenge using new strategies and methods.

How do you handle yourself, leaders, when troubles mount? Some folks double the emotional weight they place on friends. Others turn to their own strengths and bear their load with courage and fortitude. The difference is how well they have prepared themselves to cope with an increased burden. A strong spirit is not disabled by a heavy load.

One thing a leader should puzzle out in making decisions is the difference between what is possible and what is probable.

Slow down, leaders. What's the rush? Too many people hurry through life as if there were some huge, final reward for speed. The pleasures of the moment are ignored in a mad, frenzied effort to accomplish some task. It's impossible to savor the present if it's not thoroughly tasted and digested. How wise is the person who slows down before the body and mind require it.

I'm Okay, But You're a Tad Strange!

"Good luck!"

Said that to anyone recently?

Ever dreamed or thought something that later happened?

Can you make a person turn around if you stare long enough at her back?

Believe in ghosts? How about extra-terrestrial spaceships?

Do you believe some people possess telepathic ability? Now, if these questions interest you, let's try a couple more.

Do you admit to being superstitious?

Does fate seem to influence your life?

Ah, and the key one: Are you primarily a rational animal?

Actually, by your responses to this last question, you've already answered the earlier ones.

Let's try two more questions: Ever buy products because they were hawked by movie actors whose worth is valued by their ability to pretend, distort and lie? Do you believe advertising agencies are successful appealing to our objective, rational selves?

Let me describe two kinds of people. Those in the first group see themselves as objective, self-propelling, rugged individualists, thought-ful voters, discriminating consumers, and rational.

The second group are image-lovers, daydreamers, emotional, impulsive, superstitious, and irrational.

Which group do the motivation researchers, corporate social scientists, political image-makers, and advertising executives target in order to sell their products and win elections?

The answer to this question should be of considerable interest to leaders. For it not only involves our subconscious needs, beliefs and values, but focuses, as well, on the issue of rational and irrational influences and behavior.

Since World War II research in the field of psychic phenomena has obliterated demarcation lines between natural and supernatural, normal and paranormal. The distinction is now hopelessly blurred.

There have been thousands of successful experiments demonstrating extrasensory perception (ESP), which is the capacity of human beings and animals to communicate by means other than their five senses.

What's the point of all this?

How we like to see ourselves, and yet how we believe and behave, may be quite different.

We like to believe that we regulate our behavior rationally, that we are "masters of our own house." It's reassuring to believe that we are in control of how we think, believe and act.

Evidence doesn't support this thesis.

We are all primarily irrational, some more than others.

Leaders who can recognize their own irrationality will be able to understand why individuals—and especially groups—will behave irrationally at times. Most adults are not crazy or silly or foolishly obstreperous; they're just being themselves.

Leaders who believe they are rational animals usually expect others to behave in the same manner. They are in for some surprises—and perhaps shock. When people come together, irrational responses of one or two participants often encourages and galvanizes other group members to engage in similarly irrational behavior. The contagious effect has a tendency to escalate unless an adroit leader understands what is happening and can—hopefully, in a light-handed manner—encourage the group to get back on track.

Being aware that people are primarily irrational, and that groups can become even more irrational, is a giant step toward becoming more effective as a leader.

Besides, it's usually the irrationality that spices up meetings and saves the sanity of seasoned group members. Purely rational meetings, in my experience, are dull, boring, and really a huge drag. I love the strange!

Thoughts on Leadership

A leader's pride in the job he is doing should be subordinate (an appendage) to the service he's performing, and never the main theme of his position.

Leaders, be wary of those individuals whose commitment to excuses exceeds a concern for the consequences of their behavior.

Never underestimate the importance of reflection and foresight as leadership tools. The latter relies on the quality of the former.

Knowing what's important and possible, then acting on that assessment, often separates good leaders from unsuccessful ones. The latter tend to give as much attention to what is of little importance as to that which matters.

Being human means learning to live with one's own internal contradictions. A mature leader doesn't let those inconsistencies cause debilitating distress or interfere with meeting responsibilities. She works on correcting the contradictions privately, never using followers to serve her personal needs or agendas.

Interesting isn't it, that no matter how many years we serve in leadership positions, we will always be amateurs.

A Boy and a Waitress

A little boy about ten years old came into a restaurant and sat at the counter. When the waitress rushed over, the little boy asked, "How much is an ice cream sundae?"

"Fifty cents," replied the waitress.

Reaching into his pocket, he pulled out a handful of coins and carefully counted them. "How much is a dish of plain ice cream?"

With several customers waiting at the counter, the waitress was becoming impatient. "Thirty-five cents," she answered brusquely.

Again he counted the coins. "I'll have the plain ice cream," he said.

The waitress brought the ice cream, put it in front of him, accepted payment and walked away. When she came back a few minutes later, the boy was gone. She stared at the empty dish and then swallowed hard at what she saw: placed neatly beside the emptied dish were two nickels and five pennies—her tip.

The waitress still keeps the seven coins as a grateful reminder that everyone, no matter their age or size, is important. And that we all need to "take the time."

There are several lessons here for leaders: paying attention to what is really important is one of them. Paying attention to little folks and the least among us is another.

Effective leaders understand their responsibility is to serve ALL of their constituents. And, as Hubert Humphrey once remarked, the true test of their effectiveness is how well they serve those whose basic needs are the greatest.

In local communities, leaders would do well to focus more on engaging in actions that affect in positive ways citizens who are struggling to keep their lives and families together.

Remember some fifteen years ago, the lovely words of advice by Sausalito resident, Anne Herbert? "Practice random kindness and senseless acts of beauty."

Leaders usually become known for the kind of decisions that make a difference in the lives of many people. But what is often more important is the small, seemingly insignificant act of kindness that affects the life of one precious individual.

Let's be the kind of leader who never forgets the boy and the waitress.

And let's try each day to help one person and enrich one life.

Contradictions

Leaders, see if you resonate with the following:

I have spent a large part of my life struggling with contradictions.

I don't believe I'm the only one whose mind has been full of doubts, anger, confusion, fears, and outright ambivalence about matters of consequence that are neither black nor white, right nor wrong.

I mean, here I was as a child thinking simple thoughts, asking simple questions, and expecting simple answers. My world wasn't difficult to understand.

But that world changed forever when I entered school. Although I had no idea what contradictions were, I began to realize something incomprehensible was occurring to transform my simple world.

For example, my parents taught me to be good, but some kids were mean and were getting away with it, even having fun at it. I learned that honesty was the best policy, yet kids lied, cheated, stole stuff, avoided punishment, and even won the admiration of classmates. I learned that all people were equal in the eyes of God and the law, but my school was racially segregated and my classmates told nasty jokes and stories about "those people" who didn't look like us. I learned that each individual was unique; however, teachers made us learn the same thing at the same time, no matter whether we could spell or read or do math problems way beyond the lessons they were teaching. My parents and other adults conditioned me to believe that school would be exciting; much of it, I came to realize, was dull and boring.

Many adults I observed lived by the admonition, "Do as I say, not as I do." Oh, it was seldom that anyone communicated this maxim in words; rather they did it in actions. Their behavior brought this particular contradiction to life. That's still the case, of course. How often do people say one thing and do another? Politicians, I have learned, have made contradictions into an art form.

What each of us knows, I suspect, is that we inherited a whole bundle of contradictory messages from our parents, friends, teachers and other adults. When I think of the ideals we learned as youngsters and the idealism that moved us to believe in a world where goodness and justice and kindness prevail, I can only marvel that so many of us have not become certifiable cynics or authentic hypocrites.

I was instructed in hope; so far my hopes have dominated my fears, just as my idealism usually prevails over the stark, dark realities that would control my thoughts, if I let them. I live with ambiguities—always have, always will. I do not do so comfortably or indifferently. Nor, I expect, do you. That would be contrary to the picture I have of you.

So, leaders, let's acknowledge we have contradictions to deal with, that the world is chock full of more of them we haven't encountered yet, and we had better get used to the idea that this is reality—and then move on.

We have work to do!

Thoughts on Leadership

An effective leader is one who has clarified purposes and goals. This is best accomplished by writing them down. They are seldom captured or retained in an abstract form.

Some leaders mistakenly believe that in order to be serious in their endeavors they must be solemn and grim. Wrong! Serious work is best accomplished when there is balance between a frivolous, light-hearted approach and a heady, concentrated effort. An "all work and no play" attitude not only makes one dull and boring, but a pain in the patootie as well.

The more committed a leader is to projecting self-importance, the more inconsequential she will appear in the eyes of followers—who, by the way, will unlikely remain so.

Leaders, when you make a lousy decision (and you will!), acknowledge your mistake and start again. Don't compound a blunder by continuing on as if nothing happened. Character strength is built by admitting error, not by sticking to a bad decision or attempting to cover it up.

Be for yourself, of course, but be for others as well. Balance is the key. People who are only looking out for themselves, or those who profess to be only looking out for the welfare of others, cannot be fully trusted.

Self-respect is the best defense against personal attacks and the incivility of others.

The Mayor and Harmony

Once upon a time in a mountainous community, a banquet was held to honor the mayor for bringing the town through a difficult economic period to a position of prosperity.

At the center table sat the mayor with the three individuals who were most responsible for carrying out the economic recovery plan: the city manager, the director of community development, and the chair of the Citizen's Economic Outreach Committee.

At another table was John Windom, director of the Regional Leadership Institute, along with three members of his staff.

While the dinner was served, speeches given, honors bestowed, and entertainment performed, all in the large banquet hall looked on with pride and satisfaction, except for Windom's three assistants who sat dumbfounded.

Near the end of the festivities, one of them turned to John and spoke these words: "All of this seems appropriate, but to us there is an enigma."

"Please explain it to me," John responded.

"At the central table is the city manager. Clearly, without his knowledge of how other communities have confronted the crisis we had, success would have been impossible. The director of community development did most of the work, traveling to meet company executives and hosting them when they visited here. And the chair of the Citizen's Committee brought the community together and, to be sure, made this whole enterprise a public-private undertaking. Those three are responsible for bringing about our economic recovery.

What we can't understand is why the mayor is the one being primarily honored. His contributions are far less than the other three."

John smiled and asked his staff persons to imagine the wheel of an old tractor. "What determines the strength of the wheel in moving the tractor forward?" he asked.

After several minutes of conversation, one said, "It's the sturdiness of the spokes."

"Then why is it," John inquired, "two wheels made of identical spokes differ in strength?"

Seeing the confused looks on their faces, he continued. "It's important to look beyond the obvious. The wheel of an old tractor is made not only of spokes, but of space between them. Sturdy spokes poorly placed make a weak wheel. A strong wheel needs harmony between them. The essence of wheel-making lies in the craftsman's ability to conceive and create the space that holds and balances the spokes within the wheel. Look again at the head table. Who is the craftsman?"

The three understood what he was saying. But one asked a further question: "John, just how does the mayor create harmony between three such strong individuals?"

"Think of sunlight. The sun nurtures and vitalizes trees and flowers by giving away its light. And which direction do they grow? To the light, of course. This is what the mayor has done. He asked them to assume responsibilities in which they could make positive contributions and realize their potential. He then created harmony by giving them credit for their distinctive achievements. Just as the flowers and trees grow toward the sun, the individuals involved with our economic recovery grow toward the mayor with devotion. Without his light, their contributions would have been dim, indeed."

(Adapted from an Oriental parable)

Encouraging Creativity

How many times have leaders heard this kind of conversation?

"It won't work!"
"Why?"
"It just won't!"

Any leader who has spent time in organizations, or serving on volunteer boards or committees, has heard endless variations on this refrain.

All that's required is for some brave soul to suggest an innovative idea or put forth a possible solution that exceeds the experience of the group members. Negative rejoinders will roll. And because quick, faultfinding opinions so often precede thoughtful rejoinders, new ideas may be vetoed before they're even examined.

Far too many people have a propensity to focus on possible flaws rather than ask: What are the positives about the concept? What are the most interesting aspects about the idea?

Children, bless their hearts, tend to focus on the positives when something new or different is proposed. But adults are more apt to degrade or find fault. Sometimes we bury childlike ability to look creatively at fresh ideas.

One reason, I suspect, is because criticisms are easy to make. It doesn't take much skill to find flaws in new ideas. If they didn't have any defects, the idea would be perfect. Right? And few are. Also, some folks believe that leveling criticism is a form of erudition. They like to show off their intelligence and self-perceived competence as "critical thinkers."

Actually, few critics are creative. If they were, they'd focus on the interesting aspects of a new idea rather than tear it down. Creative thinkers retain the ability of the child to play with ideas, to examine strengths and minimize limitations.

And they certainly don't concern themselves with how their idea will appear to others. Fear of looking like a fool or not being regarded as a team player is a powerful excuse for refraining from submitting a new idea.

There are other barriers to creativity leaders should be sensitive to:

The pressure of time. Full meeting agendas often afford little opportunity for creative discussion or thinking about a particular idea. If a new idea is to be presented, leaders should alert and prepare participants prior to the meeting and see to it that adequate time is allotted for discussion.

Reverence for tradition and order. Creative thinkers challenge the status quo and tend to ask irreverent questions about why certain things are done a certain way. Those who provoke are more concerned with avoiding stagnation than maintaining stability. They realize that innovation and change create messes, but believe that temporary disorder may prove more beneficial than "doing things the way we've always done them."

Perceived limitation of resources. Relatively few organizational committee members or volunteer board participants are well informed in this area. When a leader, or other authority figure, explains that something can't be done because there are insufficient resources, they are unlikely to question the assessment. They don't ask "Why?" and then go on to explore alternatives. Accepting an authority's explanation is easier than pushing for creative options.

Unquestioned reliance on the group to produce answers and solutions. In every field of endeavor, some person or groups are doing the best work. Creative thinkers want to know where these "Best Practices" are and how that information can help their group. There is no need to laboriously invent a program that is functioning elsewhere. Leaders may want to learn where those programs are and who can be contacted to provide them with data that will aid in reaching decisions.

Reluctance of participants to "play." Too many people who serve on committees and boards tend to be overly serious. This is a kind way of describing most meetings as dull! The absence of a playful mood leads to the absence of creativity. The leader has choices to make about how a meeting will be conducted.

It's true, some new ideas won't work, but then there are some that might revolutionize, improve or upgrade your organization. It pays to consider each new idea positively.

And above all else, creatively.

Leaders, take note!

Thoughts on Leadership

One important part of sensitivity a leader needs to develop is to assess how much strength and support to draw from another person and to recognize when to stop drawing from that source. No one's supply of strength is inexhaustible. Too few who sap the energy of others consider replenishment.

Thank goodness for the ability to repress. Each of us is barraged by forbidden desires, hounded by the loud demands of reason and unreason, attacked by constant fears, screamed at by religious and political zealots, misled by politicians, harangued by the media, and deluged by incessant incivilities that seem to escalate daily. Leaders must find ways to bury as many of these distressful forces as possible in order to maintain sanity and accomplish the tasks before them.

A critical element in becoming a leader is temper control. Those leaders who have not learned to control their temper are examples of arrested development. Chances are there are other indications of childish behavior laying just below the surface of their personalities. Leaders, if you have a temper problem, either get professional help or stop trying to lead others.

Effective leaders who establish strong relationships are adept at picking up clues consciously and unconsciously communicated by others. What is less appreciated is the need to attend to cues. A leader is cueing consistently other's responses through verbal and nonverbal communication. Cues are usually more direct and intended than clues. They are attempts to tell the other person how to respond. A cue has a "now quality" about it.

Leaders, let me give you one more reason why it's important for you to continue to keep learning and growing. You decrease your chances of becoming a sucker for dogma. You lessen the possibility of uncritically accepting another's set of prescribed beliefs and attitudes, even when communicated strongly and with certainty. It's smart to be cautious when in the vicinity of dogmatic people.

Short-Term Thinking

Leaders, I've got this problem you can help me with.

It has to do with the kinds of decisions I see being made by leaders throughout our nation.

What disturbs me is the priority being given—increasingly, it seems to me—to short-term thinking.

It's a "what's-best-for-us-today" approach to issues.

Leaders seem to be in an inordinate hurry to respond to agendas, rush to conclusions, vote. It strikes me as a "checklist" mentality. "There are twelve items before us today, folks, so let's see how quickly we can dispense with them."

And everyone acquiesces, no matter how complex the issues and far-reaching the consequences may be.

Well, you see, that's when someone ought to be asking questions. But the preference is to move as quickly and expeditiously as possible right to a decision. The problem with this strategy is threefold: the tendency to respond only to immediate and apparent exigencies; the tendency to trust others' judgments rather than one's own; the tendency to fail to examine in depth the ramifications of the decision.

Now it's pretty clear that leaders in reasonably important positions are conditioned to reach conclusions quickly. "Getting things done" is usually part of their qualifications. And, often, this particular strategy works—but not always.

But that's only part of the point. Does the decision-making process take others with them? And have the leaders given adequate attention to questions?

I am sympathetic to leaders who are somewhat put off by questions. Ask a question and you know that some people are pathologically incapable of providing a brief response. It's true there are those who cannot be content with a "yes/no" answer. They feel compelled to provide a boring history or an abstract dissertation on all possible connections, or they insert seemingly endless autobiographical stories that have little relation to the problem at hand.

Yes, questions can sometimes be downers.

But, when attempting to render decisions that affect the lives of others, questions about long-term consequences should be encouraged and asked. And that's not being handled very well these days.

Perhaps there is a need to adopt the perspective of the Senecas. Before the tribe made decisions, the elders would ask the question: "How will this affect the next seven generations?"

Now, that approach truly makes one stop and think!

Leaders and Psychological Contracts

What, you may ask, are psychological contracts?

Well, I respond, they are the hidden roots under every interpersonal exchange. When two people communicate, unspoken expectations of one another are rarely identical. Misunderstanding and conflict may result.

Put bluntly, leaders, if you don't want to screw up your relationships with others, and if you do want to improve your ability to be an effective leader, you need to pay close attention to psychological contracts.

Okay? Let's begin examining this fascinating and critically important topic, which, by the way, was initially developed at The Menninger Foundation.

Now, I'm going to write about this subject but you need to know right off that I know absolutely nothing about it and you are a fool to read beyond this sentence!

What an outrageous statement? Right?

I purposely violated your psychological contract with me, the author.

My implied contract goes like this:

> *"I, the author, have written something that is worth your reading. You, the reader, will be better informed (educated, amused, etc.,) by having read it."*

Conversely, your psychological contract goes something like this:

"I, the reader, believe the writer has written something worthwhile, and I am going to take some of my precious time to read it. I hope to be better informed (educated, amused, etc.,) by reading it."

Now the fact is, no author or publisher ever requires you to sign a written contract pledging that you will read a book through to completion, or that you will pass a written test at the end or be charged double, just as you don't hold the author accountable for ensuring that you are better informed (educated, amused, etc.,) by virtue of having read the book. A written contract would be ludicrous. But a psychological contract exists.

The psychological contract is real. In one way or another, it's at the heart of every interaction. It causes a lot more problems than legal contracts, primarily because it gets violated so often. Most of the time when we foul up in our interpersonal relationships, it's because we violated a psychological contract.

Legal contracts are easy to recognize. They are written, clauses are clearly presented, and a final agreement is reached only when the expectations of both parties are reciprocal and mutually understood. Signatures are required after a period of careful and precise negotiations.

Not so with psychological contracts. There is no precise, careful, explicit period of negotiation. Quite the contrary. Psychological contracts are unwritten, nonverbal, and often unconscious expectations that underlie every relationship we have. They constitute what you expect of another person. And since they are unspoken and unwritten, it's unlikely the other person is aware of them.

That's where the rub comes in. Your version of your psychological contract with me may be quite different from mine with you.

Interestingly enough, neither of us is likely to discover that our expectations differ until one of us violates the contract.

What follows is an attempt to illuminate the kinds of psychological contracts each of us experiences in our lives, their characteristics, and how they might be better understood and managed. Hopefully, leaders, when you finish this section, you'll feel equipped to deal more effectively, knowledgeably, and confidently with the expectations you and others have about each other.

Early Conditioning

To comprehend what psychological contracts are about, let's start at the beginning with a hypothetical example that may ring true:

> *"I am your baby. I didn't ask to be here but since I am, I want you to take care of me, love me, hold me, change my diapers when they get wet or dirty, feed me, and pay attention when I cry. You do these things for me and I think we'll get along pretty well."*

> *"I am your mother. I will love you, hold you, change you, feed you, and respond to you when you cry. In return I want you to love me, let me play with you, learn to smile for me, and I will try to be a good mother."*

> *"Welcome son. I am your daddy. I will love you, and bring you little presents. I will not change your diapers or feed you, and I will begin teaching you how to be a 'real boy.'"*

Obviously, in these earliest of psychological contracts there are some interesting issues surfacing. The baby expects to be well cared for and will let someone (anyone!) know when he is not receiving the treatment he wants. Mother has agreed to satisfy the baby's needs, while good old dad has carved out a traditional stereotypical role to satisfy his own needs. As indicated earlier, this psychological contract will work until one of the parties feels violated.

> *"How come it's always me who has to get up in the middle of the night to feed him and change his diapers?"*

"Because that's a mother's job; that's how come!"

At this point, either their positions polarize and their relationship continues with mom resentfully performing her motherly role, or the two of them re-negotiate the agreement with dad becoming more of an active parent. But once the problem is verbalized and put out in the open, it ceases to be a psychological contract.

In other words, a major characteristic of the psychological contract is that it's unspoken. Once verbalized, the psychological contract is no more!

But let's return to the psychological contract dialogue. Daddy has taken the position that he will not do "motherly" work but will teach junior how to be a "real boy." If allowed to continue, this psychological contract will have a profound effect upon the youngster. He will be conditioned to believe that mothers (women) perform certain functions and fathers (men) perform others. Women nurture, men do not. Women like cuddly babies, fathers like real boys. This psychological contract has done as much to perpetuate the chauvinistic role as any conditioned learning pattern.

What else is occurring in this dialogue sequence? Since the baby soon will become a young boy and is unaware of the psychological contract between his father and himself, he doesn't realize what is expected of him to become the real boy his father has fashioned for him. From his father, he learns to defend himself against others, not to cry or show his emotions, to stand on his own two feet, to play with action-packed video games and guns, and throw a football. He learns to do the things that dad believes real boys must know in order to become "real men."

Obviously, this psychological contract between father and son gets more complicated if mom seeks to pursue actively her psychological contract with the boy. She feels a son should elevate cleanliness, proper language, courtesy, good manners, and helping with household chores; she supports his need to cry, to hug, to be held. While she is nurturing the feminine side of the child, the father is demeaning those characteristics by elevating his masculine side at the expense of the feminine.

The youngster is clearly caught in the middle. He is expected to live up to two sets of ideals that are never explained to him. He receives one set of guidelines from his father, another from his mother. While I use the son example here, the reader should understand the example of a daughter could also be drawn with another set of interesting variations. Listen to the soliloquy "Bill" in the musical *Carousel* to hear a prospective father's interpretation of his role with each gender.

Underlying this clash of parents with each other is their joint psychological contract with the youngster: that the boy should surpass them. "*In order for our lives to have real meaning, junior should have all the advantages we didn't have, go beyond our limitations, live out all of our unconscious fantasies and hopes and dreams that we didn't achieve.*"

It's precisely because the most critical parts of the psychological contract are unconscious that the youngster finds himself faced with the incredibly difficult task of living up to ideals that are never explained. This is further complicated because, while there is mutual need in any parent–child relationship, the needs of the child are open to control and manipulation by the parents. They are more obvious, whereas the needs of the parents tend to be hidden.

In addition, parents have progressed through the growth and development stages the young person is experiencing and, thus, believe they know what is best for the child. The father *knows* the real boy must become a real man, and to do so he must learn certain things and act in certain ways. Father knows best! Since the child has little perspective on his growth and development, he is likely to follow the guidelines set down by his most important male role model.

The problem becomes more complex because the guidelines keep changing. Each child becomes a different person at different stages of his development. Yet the parent remains relatively stable throughout these stages, trying to make sense out of the youngster's changing attitudes and behavior. In trying to keep up with the youngster, parents must constantly adjust their psychological contracts to accommodate the maturation of the offspring. Inevitably, there is difficulty in adjusting quickly and accurately enough to maintain a positive relationship. The agreement they felt worked well with the youngster last week may not work satisfactorily today. Many of the parent-advice columns are centered on helping parents understand how to adapt to these changing psychological contracts. The parent operates on one set of assumptions, the young person on another. As long as they remain unspoken, there will be problems.

Spousal Contracts

When a couple marries, they each bring with them differing psychological contracts. It's no exaggeration to say that most family problems revolve around this volatile issue.

Over fifty years ago I entered into a major psychological contract about which I have been learning since. It began with marriage vows. When I spoke the words, "I shall love, honor and cherish...," little did I realize what I had gotten myself into. Here I was, a young man, experienced in dealing with only one woman (my mother) and very few girls, who was entering into a pledge with almost all the fine print unknown to me. I have spent fifty-plus years discovering what that inexperienced kid committed me to.

Of course, that girl, who had experience with only two men (her father and older brother), and as she told me, "Oh, very few boys," (Hah!) has spent those same fifty-plus years discovering what she somehow got committed to. As with every union, we have had painful, humorous, exasperating times bringing to light the contractual agreements underlying the relationship.

A friend of mine revealed another fascinating psychological contract situation. He and his wife were on a business trip together during which he interviewed candidates for a position in his firm. As he described to his wife an interview with an impressive prospect who had confronted forcefully and publicly an unscrupulous individual, she interrupted to exclaim, "You know, I just realized something. You're not a very nice person!" Needless to say this provoked a heated discussion. For seven years she had expected her husband to behave as her mother, father, brother, and friends had behaved: nice, likable, and non-confrontational. On the other hand, his commitment was to be honest and forthright. Further, he expected his wife to be honest; niceness was not a high priority to him. They were forced to re-negotiate their psychological contract.

An advice columnist letter is illustrative. A woman wrote that her husband of two years didn't treat her as a wife but as a mother. She complained that he wanted to be comforted whenever any little thing went wrong, to pick up his clothes which he left all over the house, to select his clothes and see that he was properly dressed, and to even help him wash his ears out and clip his hair. She wanted to be a wife; he wanted a mother.

These examples illustrate that not all husbands and wives live by the same contract. Every couple has a number of different unspoken expectations which cause problems as the weeks, months, and years of marriage build up. As children join the family unit, additional psychological contracts will be established. Again, a psychological contract will work until one of the parties feels violated; one's expectation of the other is challenged.

Contracts In Organizations

Whenever two people come together, psychological contracts exist. Whenever an employee and an organization come together, this is also true. Psychological contract negotiations begin with the very first contact between a potential employee and the organization.

In the initial interview there is usually a formal verbalized conversation about the potential employee's job history, background, goals, salary, benefits, job description, and expectations. Simultaneously, there is the informal sub rosa mutual evaluation taking place as each party tests how they feel about the other. Each is sifting through the veil of words to determine how the "fit" will work, if at all. Interestingly enough, a potential employee and interviewer already have unspoken expectations about the other before they sit down together. Representing the organization, the interviewer knows what kind of person to look for, how the individual might fit into the organizational culture. Likewise, the potential employee has certain preconceived ideas about how an organization should function and how this organization in particular should respond to him.

Suppose, for instance, the organization was looking for potential leaders who would put their jobs at the top of the priority ladder, who would work whatever number of hours a day it took to get the job done, who would take special travel assignments for weeks at a time; no demand would be too great. Then suppose the potential employee was a committed family person, wanting a balanced life, with time to enjoy being with his wife and children. The match wouldn't be made because no psychological contract could bond such different expectations.

Within the internal workings of every organization, many psychological contracts exist. Here's one I remember well:

> *Some years ago as a university professor, I decided that the most effective way to teach students was to enter into a contract with them. I agreed that I'd provide them with certain knowledge I possessed, and in return they would provide me with a pledge to perform certain tasks that would contribute to their learning and expand my knowledge as well. In other words, we agreed that our time together would be mutually rewarding; that neither of us would take up the other's time in boring, dull, meaningless activity.*

> *In the context of this contract, it was clear that each of us wanted something from the other and each of us indicated we would try to provide what the other wanted.*

As I entered into these stated contracts, I began to compare them with the standard psychological contracts between teachers and students. The usual psychological contract runs like this: *"You are in my classroom (teacher to student) so you will do as I want you to do. Your task is to learn and my task is to teach. Your job is to figure out what I know and confirm what I know. I have the questions and the answers and your task is to provide me the answers (which I already know) to the questions I ask. Although the learning process is indeed an active one, your assignment is to be quiet and passive in my classroom unless I permit you to speak or move around."*

Few teachers, of course, will come out and verbally identify this kind of contract, but students learn quickly in their academic experience that understanding such contracts and acting accordingly are vital to their success. Exceptions are quickly noted.

Here's another example from one of my earlier lives:

> *During the early and mid-sixties, at the height of the civil rights movement, I taught at a black university in Alabama and was involved in teaching and administration at a white university in Iowa. During this period, I observed a fascinating psychological contract shift. Up until the mid or late sixties, a very clear psychological contract existed in almost all organizations that went like this: if two people were competing for the same job, one white, one black, the white person got the job. I was intrigued as I watched the psychological contract shift occurring. It went from the above with the white person getting the jobs if both were equally qualified, to the black getting some jobs even when the white was better qualified.*

Affirmative action played a part, but so did the changing psychological contracts. This changing approach to the work place brought on, predictably, considerable anger from white employees, which previously, of course, was the primary emotion blacks carried within them as they confronted the injustice of work place practices.

Until the mid-sixties the psychological contract was clear: white men were considered more valuable and thus deserved preference. In a relatively short period of time, blacks became more valuable. And white workers who had been conditioned to view themselves as the favored sons, felt betrayed. They expressed their anger by quitting, acts of sabotage, or at the very least, vociferous bitching.

The traditional psychological contract had been broken. A new psychological contract began to emerge that said "they" (blacks, Puerto Ricans, Hispanics, women) would receive equal treatment in job hiring while many white males were reeling from this reversal—and still are!

An organization has its own, unique set of psychological contracts as does each individual. Obviously, there will never be a perfect match. But two things are critical if the match is to work: the employee and the organization should learn as much as possible about each other before mating, and once wed the employee should ferret out and be prepared to adapt to the organizational psychological contracts. Power generally determines who does the adapting.

Characteristics of Psychological Contracts

Psychological Contracts Are Unspoken

Four basic characteristics of psychological contracts can be identified. First, as indicated earlier, they consist of **unspoken expectations.**

Let's take a look at other examples:

When I was a student and later a professor, one of the unspoken expectations I worked under was that it was okay to be tested or test students on a Friday, but it was somehow a violation to retest

> *them over the same information the following Monday. Indeed,*
> *"pop" quizzes have always been judged unfair by students. They*
> *violate the way the game is played.*

I used to do seminars for and speeches to leaders around the country. Each time I mounted a platform to speak, my psychological contract would be something like this:

> *I will be an active presenter and you are permitted to be passive*
> *participants. I will present information and you will listen. I will*
> *not embarrass you by asking you to summarize my presentation,*
> *answer tough questions, or share with the group troubling personal*
> *problems.*

The leaders I spoke to understood their psychological contract as:

> *The presenter will be active and I can be as passive as I want. If I*
> *feel like it, I will ask questions or contribute my knowledge or*
> *express my opinion, but I will determine when and what I will*
> *offer to the group.*

Obviously, I could break the psychological contract anytime by trying to force participants into an active role. But unless the pre-seminar material indicated there would be group-speaker interaction, or I made this clear in my opening remarks, there would likely be anger and resentment because I violated the psychological contract.

Another highly visible psychological contract exists in elevators. I love to observe the behavior of people in crowded elevators, but even more joyous is to violate the elevator psychological contract. This is a snap to do: Just begin talking to people. Or if feeling unusually sadistic, step in and don't turn around. Just look at people—and smile! Not only will you stop all conversation, but you'll likely force some ill-at-ease occupants to evacuate the cell at earlier floors than their intended destination.

The point is, each of us operates under a huge number of unspoken, non-verbalized expectations with the many people we encounter during our lives. The more contact we have with a person, the more psychological contracts we develop and, inevitably, the more need there is to explicate many of these expectations into clearly identifiable agreements.

Psychological Contracts Antedate

The second characteristic of psychological contracts is that they **antedate formal, signed contracts and relationships**. The individuals involved bring to any situation or relationship expectations from their past. Even though these expectations were developed before the two parties met, nevertheless they are more powerful than the demands of the written contract and present relationship.

Returning to our earlier example, the mother had a set of expectations about her baby before she gave birth. Just as she had prior expectations of how she as a mother should behave and how her husband should perform his fathering responsibilities, her husband had prior expectations about the baby, his wife and himself.

"Because that's a mother's job, that's how come!" is a statement that, no doubt, developed in his mind long before he met his wife. It was there, but it took her question, *"How come it's always me who has to get up in the middle of the night to feed him and change his diapers?"* to bring it out.

Each wife—and husband—has expectations of how a spouse should behave long before the wedding takes place. Remember the advice column letter? Recall my friend's psychological contract with his wife about being "nice?" Here's another example:

> *Years ago I inherited a secretary considerably older than I and much more experienced in her job than I was in mine. Although a rather young (chronologically) administrator, I did feel confident about my abilities to discharge responsibilities in a competent*

manner. As I settled into assignments, I realized that I had two "bosses; one official and one unofficial; the latter being the secretary, of course. Not only was she instructing me how to do my job, but dictated memos and letters came back to me to sign significantly altered from my original words. It didn't take long to understand what was really going on. We were operating under different psychological contracts.

Hers went like this:

"I am older, more experienced and have worked in this office longer than you. Therefore, I know more about your job than you do and can do it better than you can. Besides, the previous occupant of your office was lazy, so I did his job for him, just as I will do yours."

My psychological contract was:

"I have been assigned a set of responsibilities which I need to do in my own way. I am in charge; you are here to assist and support me to the best of your ability. For better or for worse, I will make the necessary decisions."

To shorten a tedious story, I began to articulate the psychological contract. She acknowledged her prior expectations, but in doing so, discovered that she couldn't work for me. I helped her transfer to another division where, I hope, she and her boss lived happily ever after.

Psychological Contracts Are Dynamic

Psychological contracts **change; they are dynamic**. The changes they undergo depend on the situation and the needs of the parties involved. In this regard, a psychological contract is quite different from a written contract which enforces permanency to the initial agreement between the contractual parties.

All of us face major problems with the changing nature of psychological contracts. While accustomed to the permanent and binding characteristics of written contracts, we must try to adapt to psychological contracts which will continually change as the relationships change. This is no easy task. Remember the earlier example about the changing psychological contracts between whites and minorities? Here's another one:

> *Back in the seventies, in my small but growing business, I employed a man with whom I'd earlier worked closely for several years. He was an excellent performer and we discussed many times how pleased we were with each other and how much he enjoyed his job and the organization. As the company expanded, I hired another person to assume some of my responsibilities. The nature of our jobs dictated that we work together much of each day, especially during the first several months.*
>
> *Imagine my surprise when the first man walked into my office to tell me he was resigning his position. Swallowing my shock, we talked. What emerged was this: He felt "left out" and abandoned by me; he was no longer important to me or the company because I spent so little time with him; he was deeply hurt that our relationship had deteriorated to the point where I no longer needed him.*
>
> *I explained that this certainly wasn't the case. I told him that I felt his performance was superior, that I missed our previously close working relationship but a) he no longer needed my daily supervision since was very capable of independently managing his responsibilities, and b) I had to spend time with the new person to assist her to learn her job.*

What emerged was the verbalization of a psychological contract in which he expected that I would like him better and, thus, would continue to want to spend time together in a close working relationship. He was going to resign because he felt I was violating an agreement—a psychological contract I didn't know existed. Once discussed openly, he was able to laugh at his irrational (and painful) behavior and acknowledge that he certainly wasn't justified in resigning. I admitted that I probably paved the way by not explaining to him that we would no longer be able to spend so much time together.

In organizations, psychological contracts are constantly changing because there are so many of them. In my experience, the most frequent cause of interpersonal problems and resignations is the violation of psychological contracts between managers and subordinates; there is no way to be aware of all the expectations others have of you. This reality is compounded by the fact that even when a psychological contract is exposed and discussed, it will probably change. The closer the relationship, the more difficult the psychological contract to cope with.

Within Psychological Contracts, There is Mutual Recognition of Need

Mutual recognition of need is an awareness that each party needs the other. The child needs a parent, just as a parent needs the child. A follower needs a leader, but a leader without followers is no leader at all. An employee needs an employer, but an employer cannot function without employees. In organizations there needs to be a mutual recognition that the workers need the organization to be efficient, productive and care about their welfare, while the organization needs the employees to cooperate, hone their skills, and work toward organizational goals.

When psychological contracts work well in an organization, mutual expectations are met and each side of the contract recognizes its need for the other. Companies tend to attract people who will be comfortable there. As such people are attracted, they add to the qualities that attracted them in the first place. These people make the organization even more like itself until the organization begins to take on a personality of its own.

Further, the reason why the organization becomes a single identity is because those persons who interview prospective employees tend to hire in their own image. The mutual recognition issue is extended in a very real way: "We need you because you look and think and behave as we do, and you need us because you'll be comfortable with us."

Interestingly, it's this mutual recognition issue that lies at the heart of strikes. So long as there is the recognition that each party needs the other, strikes are unlikely to occur. From a psychological point of view, strikes occur when employees perceive that management doesn't need them anymore. When examined carefully, it's often discovered that, in one way or another, management *has* conveyed the message that they can get along without the employees, or at least some of them. If organizational leaders would pay more careful attention to this extraordinarily significant psychological contract characteristic, there would likely be fewer strikes.

This fourth characteristic rests, then, upon the assumption of mutual need. If you and I did not need each other in some way or for some reason, then there is no reason for a contract between us. A psychological contract will not work unless each party has something to give and something to gain. With many psychological contracts, one must look closely to see the mutual need because the need isn't always obvious; it's easy to get fooled. For instance, it's clear that the patient needs the therapist. It's less obvious that the therapist can only help the person who needs and wants their help.

When mutual recognition of need is understood, both parties will—for the most part—be equally satisfied and satisfying. When this occurs, the result is reciprocation. Each party honors the needs of the other and becomes adapting to the other's needs. It is fascinating to watch the selfish baby grow into a young child who, albeit in stumbling, awkward but lovable ways, tries to meet the needs of her parents by crawling to them, smiling, playing with them, and later giving them small gifts such as a teddy or blanket. Reciprocation is haltingly but inexorably learned. In the early years of marriage it's especially important to learn and practice reciprocation. Giving and receiving expressions of love is a matter of recognizing mutual need.

Managing Psychological Contracts

As two parties come together, psychological contracts develop. When expectations between them are unclear, misunderstanding, confusion, and chronic dissatisfaction are constant threats. The primary task in managing psychological contracts is to do the best job you can to become aware of the contracts you have with others and with your organization. Recognition that they exist is the first critical step. The second step is to work at making the psychological contracts explicit; try to understand the ramifications and conditions involved. Third, work at negotiating the contracts carefully with the other party involved. In coping realistically with psychological contracts, you must accept the fact that the psychological needs underlying the psychological contracts are real and legitimate, to you and the other party. By the time you have made them clear and negotiated with the other party, they are no longer psychological contracts, but verbal agreements.

Keep in mind that whenever a psychological contract exists, there are two components which may represent varying needs. There will likely be disagreement surrounding viewpoints. Rather than denying conflict or trying avoidance maneuvers, it's better to confront it by verbalizing the unspoken expectations. Once spoken, you're likely to discover the expectations have lost their demanding quality and have become invitations to negotiate.

Be reminded that conflict in itself is neither positive nor negative; it's mishandling conflict that causes problems. Unspoken conflicts tend not to disappear but rather to fester until broken open by a provocation or disagreement, which usually results in unpleasant consequences. Better to foster an environment of open communication in which psychological contracts are brought to the surface and examined before they build up into serious conflicts that become more difficult to resolve. While conflict may be stressful, it's unlikely to become distressful unless allowed to remain unexamined. Only occasionally are open, well-defined conflicts distressful.

The psychological contract can be examined and worked with from the very first encounter between two parties. For example, when interviewing a job applicant, ask about her attitude toward change. See how comfortable both of you are as you discuss issues that bring you psychologically closer or more distant. Help the individual express expectations about the organization and try tactfully to put your, and the organization's, expectations, into words. Let the prospective employee know that you recognize there will be mutual needs in the relationship.

In establishing healthy psychological contracts, work toward developing interdependent relationships. "I feel comfortable being dependent upon you if I know later you will use me in the same way." In this approach neither person needs to feel guilty for using the other. The more we function in the interdependent manner, the more trusting we become that neither of us will exploit the other's dependency.

The same relationship should be nurtured between an employee and the organization. When you join an organization, you are agreeing to give up some freedom in order to receive support. When the support you receive is not reasonably commensurate with the freedom you've given up, you may resign your job. This is also true in relationships and marriages. Interdependence occurs when the tradeoffs are reasonably equal. Neither party wants to give support all the time without receiving some in return, just as neither wants to give up freedom without getting support. As an employee, it's important for you to know that you don't share all of the dependence in the relationship with your organization, but that your employer depends on and needs you just as much as you need him.

Another vital step in managing psychological contracts is self-knowledge. The better you understand yourself, the better will you understand the psychological contracts that affect your relationships. Ask yourself these questions: What are the major psychological contracts between my spouse and me? What psychological contracts govern my relationship with my employer? What are the primary psychological contracts between my coworkers and me? Between me and those I serve? Between my children and me?

Finally, to better manage psychological contracts, work to develop empathy—try to put yourself in the other person's position. Ask yourself, "What is it like to be her? If I were leading this organization, what would I do? How would I behave?" Two essential keys to unlocking psychological contracts are self-awareness and empathy. Continue the fascinating task of learning as much about yourself as you can while simultaneously expending the effort and energy of learning about the people with whom you share primary relationships. You will never discover all the psychological contracts under which you and others operate, but the adventure of searching for and discovering them will be exciting and revealing. Psychological contracts are never boring.

Thoughts on Leadership

When we don't understand something, there is a strong tendency to oppose it. Leaders must take the time and make the effort to understand the issues to be placed in front of their followers, then determine how best to explain them.

Leaders will discover there is a fine line between their perseverance and other folks' pigheadedness.

A leader's personal qualities should provide her with honor comparable to that which she achieves through her work in an elected or professional position. A truly significant leader takes at least as much satisfaction in trying to be a good person as in reaping the benefits of success in office or career.

Without a well-developed sense of humor, a leader is like a car without springs—he's going to be uncomfortable every time he hits a bump.

Perhaps the best measure of how successful a leader has been in her life, is not what she has done for others, but what others have done because of her. Infusing a spark, or better yet, a spirit, into another person, ensures that her life will live on in others.

◇◇◇

Blessed is the leader who, in her mature years, still regards HOPE as the memory of the future.

The Professor and the Centipede

During the sixteen years I spent as an administrator and professor in several universities and colleges, I heard many wonderful stories that have important implications for leaders.

Here's one of my favorites.

It seems this research professor applied for, and received, a major government grant to study the behavior of centipedes. The good doctor (Ph.D., by the way) hypothesized that examining the behavior of this small critter would enable him to extrapolate data that would better explain the continuing bizarre behavior of two-legged creatures called humans.

The funds from Washington arrived in the university president's office and were duly transferred, amid triplicate forms and mountainous piles of substantiating records, to the professor's laboratory, which he had set up under the conditions of a previous grant in which he had studied the mating techniques of moth larvae.

Grant in hand, he set about collecting centipedes and when he had fifty or so in cages, he began his study—or experiment, as he preferred to call it.

First, he carefully removed the centipede from the cage, set in on the lab table, then loudly clapped his hands together just behind the critter. The poor centipede jumped inches forward. The professor was elated.

He replicated the experiment with the others. Then, satisfied that he was on to something, he pulled out the first centipede and proceeded to clip off two of the little critter's legs. He then emphatically clapped his hands again behind the creature and again the centipede jumped forward, although not as far as it did the first time, the professor noted.

He repeated the process again and again with the critters, recording the same results with each one. Then, he cut two more legs off the first centipede, noted that it jumped a lesser distance after he clapped, and so on and so on until he had severed all but two of the legs off each centipede.

This was the big moment he had been working toward. Rubbing his hands together so they would not sting when he brought them harshly together, he then took a deep breath and clapped his hands as loudly as possible behind the first poor creature. The centipede didn't move at all. Exhilarated, the professor repeated this final phase of the experiment with every critter. The results were the same.

The professor was extremely excited. His hypothesis was proven; the experiment was a resounding success. Thus, he wrote his great academic paper, concluding in the final sentence of the final paragraph that, "the evidence is incontrovertible that when all the legs of the centipede are cut off, the creature becomes completely deaf."

The moral here has something to do with checking assumptions, doesn't it? Perhaps you believe I could have made this point without the story—and you're probably right.

But, look for a moment at this matter of assumptions again. You assume you would remember the importance of "checking your assumptions" when planning and discharging leadership responsibilities if I simply and cogently suggested you do so.

I, on the other hand, believe that checking your assumptions when planning to lead a group is so important that I used this long story to help you remember as well as to emphasize how critical this issue is to the successful undertaking of a leadership function.

Who is right?

I don't know, but I assume you'll find out as time goes by!

Thoughts on Leadership

Leaders, if you ever hear yourself make statements like, "I don't know why I did that," or "That just wasn't me," the chances are pretty good that you need to become better acquainted with yourself.

One way of evaluating the health and welfare of a community or society is by observing whether leaders exhibit compassion—and initiate corrective action—for those citizens whose futures are bleak. How a leader serves those in need is not primarily a political statement, but a reflection of that person's soul. To serve the wealthy and influential while neglecting the poorest among us indicates a soul lacking in basic humanity.

I will never vote for a person who develops an "enemies" list. Their small minds are matched by their mean-spiritedness and impoverished souls.

Alibis are self-enhancing rationalizations connected to a self-serving imagination. Don't go there, leaders.

When leaders do not know what they don't know, the organizations they serve are headed for serious trouble.

Separating reason from rationalization is a lifelong challenge for leaders. It should always receive high priority status.

Handling Your Aggression

Leaders, if someone calls you aggressive, are you likely to take offense?

I hope not. There is nothing wrong with being aggressive; it's how you handle your aggression that can get you in trouble.

To be successful in any endeavor, you must be aggressive. That's true for business executives, managers, students, athletes, parents, children, and certainly for leaders.

It's even true for babies. As a fetus, baby, and healthy child, the little individual is an aggressive bundle of energy. Likewise a healthy adult is an aggressive adult.

Why is it, then, that so many folks regard aggression as negative or dangerous? One reason is fear of its spontaneity: it can suddenly break out and we fear loss of control. Another reason is lack of positive outlets against which to discharge aggressive drives. Put differently, far too many people haven't learned how to redirect their aggression into harmless channels.

For instance, I used to play competitive tennis. Playing the game was a marvelous therapeutic redirection for me. Some of my friends were astonished to see this normally thoughtful, calm, controlled, kind (okay, so I'm stretching it!) person try to rip some poor guy apart on the tennis court. An hour there was far better for me than screaming at my wife—and a whole lot safer.

So, participating in—and even watching—sporting events is a healthy way of unloading aggression.

Road rage is not!

Clearly, there are socially acceptable ways of discharging aggression as well as socially unacceptable ways. The challenge is to discover and use the former while minimizing the latter.

Unfortunately, we receive mixed messages about aggression. We live in a society filled with intense and insane social violence on the one hand and taboos against the expression of even the simplest emotions of personal aggression on the other. This ethic has created a peculiar double standard that it's okay to enjoy cruelty and viciousness in anonymous, vicarious ways, but expression of face-to-face aggression is bad.

No wonder we look for ways to pray it or play it away.

The key is to find the means to express our aggression in normal, healthy ways that work for us. This is a primary way of staying alive and healthy. We are more likely to become ill when our aggressive drives are diminished or lacking. Similarly, full mobilization of aggression is required for the recovery from illness. Persons who maintain an aggressive fight toward recovery stand a much better chance of surviving severe illness.

So, leaders, enjoy your aggression. And keep in mind that worthwhile tasks, creative endeavors, and organizational achievements are best accomplished by constructive, aggressive action. To be successful, be aggressive.

Go for it, leaders!

Nice People

If you place a high value on being liked, I suggest you not apply for leadership positions where confrontation and argumentation are probable. School boards and town/city councils are examples. Decisions, for sure, won't please everyone, and some folks are likely to take your name in vain.

Of course, I also suggest you try to find more satisfaction in being respected than liked—but that's whole separate topic.

Another characteristic incompatible with disputatious positions is NICENESS. Now, don't misunderstand. I'm not talking about Aunt Harriet or Cousin John or even Mother Matilda. They're probably very nice, but not NICE! I'm referring to those people who never get their dander up, avoid making hard choices, lack firmness in the face of hostility, and are uncomfortable dealing with disagreements. They are always smiling, ever cheerful, a good word for everyone, a serenity that provokes awe, and a sweetness that makes diabetics nauseous.

In other words, their behavior is unreal. And their NICENESS has a price—for you and for them. NICE behavior can be alienating, indirectly hostile, and self-destructive. Why? Read on.

First of all, the NICE person holds his aggression in. Everyone is aggressive at times, but the NICE individual can't let his aggressions show. He keeps it inside which is likely to result in psychosomatic problems like headaches and ulcers. A possible psychological result is alienation as others become uneasy with the person's attitude and approach to them.

Second, the uneasiness one feels around the NICE person limits relationships because of having to be on guard. You never know if the NICE person can handle conflict or sustain an angry confrontation, especially if it occurs spontaneously.

Third, the NICE person tends to create an atmosphere that prevents others from giving her honest, genuine feedback. Usually she doesn't want feedback because her plate is already filled with "niceties" that are needed to maintain her approach to life. Unfortunately, lack of feedback blocks her emotional growth while sustaining her self-portrait.

Fourth, NICE behavior is distrusted by others. How do you know the NICE person will come to your aid in a crisis situation that requires a confrontation with others?

Fifth, NICE people stifle growth. Since they avoid giving genuine feedback, they deprive others of a real person to bounce against. You can feel massive guilt if you get angry at a NICE person.

There's more, of course, but the bottom line is that NICE people do not become effective leaders. Why? Because their behavior is unreliable and emotionally counterfeit. An individual in a leadership position cannot always make NICE decisions that demonstrate their "niceness" for others to admire. Leadership requires a variety of faces; the smiling, serene countenance that only offers soft, soothing platitudes is much too limited, restrictive, and inauthentic.

Thoughts on Leadership

The older leaders become, the more they tend to hear only what they want to hear. It's what they do not wish to know about themselves that increasingly defines their success or failure as a leader—and as a person. The internal, often unconscious, barriers they erect to prevent themselves from receiving information that threatens their preferred self-identity, act as active and effective censors. Consequently, they ignore or repress potentially helpful truths that might correct behavior flaws or rectify relationship problems. The statement, "I'm too old to change," is sometimes an acknowledgment that the leader is determined to shut out information that doesn't fit his self-image.

Leaders, try to understand and be patient with people who feel little or no pride in their own identity. These folks will often associate themselves with a noble cause, respected organization, or admired leader. They will then trumpet the special qualities of the cause, organization or leader, thus proclaiming their own worth through the association. It's an easy way to establish one's apparent superiority to others without making difficult sacrifices and undertaking long-term personal growth transformations.

Any significant shift in one's identity involves a spiritual shift. Any perceived identity change that doesn't involve the soul is play-acting.

Life is, of course, full of trivialities. How admirable are leaders who overcome the seductive pull of being satisfied with superficial attractions.

Leaders will inevitably have contact with self-righteous individuals. So, they should be aware that inside that person is a sense of worthlessness. They need your patience, understanding, and if they are open to it, your help.

Patience—It's Overrated

Most leaders believe patience is something to be cultivated; that it's a positive characteristic. I think it has a downside. Read on!

A friend and I recently sat through an incredibly boring speech delivered by a man who either had nothing to say or seriously underestimated his audience.

The following day we compared notes. He thought the speech was okay; he just didn't like the ending.

"What was wrong with it?" I asked.

"It was too far from the beginning," he replied.

Our conversation then turned to the subject of patience. Since neither of us is blessed with a full tank, we decided it's possession is way overrated.

We agreed that patience can be a virtue in some instances, but not in others.

I can be patient with some people and not with others. In the latter category, I have trouble with people whose interest in a topic extends no further than the end of their sentence. Or people who speak down to me. Or people who think their truths are God-given.

You get the picture.

Patience is no virtue when injustice prevails, or when you must right immediate wrongs, or when accidents are imminent, or when stupidity is about to carry a bad decision to action.

Then there's the misinterpreted patience of friendship, which often passes as loving tolerance. Letting a friend commit dumb or dangerous acts because "After all, we're friends," is to misunderstand friendship.

To be a true friend, you must be willing to risk friendship. "I care about you so much that I will risk our friendship in order to prevent you from doing this dangerous act."

Uncaring patience with a friend may result in his hurting or killing himself or others.

Part of our dilemma about patience relates to a misunderstanding of conflict. Most people learn that it's bad, or at least something to avoid when interacting with others.

Nonsense! As with aggression, so it is with conflict. It's *how we handle it* that can cause problems.

Entering into conflict with a friend may forestall more serious problems, when patience only would exacerbate the problems.

So, leaders, I suggest you not look on "patience" as an absolute. It can be a virtue or a downer. It depends.

Quick Fixes

Listen, leaders, for just a moment, to the wisdom of Oliver Wendell Holmes: "I wouldn't give a fig for the simplicity on this side of complexity; I would give my right arm for the simplicity on the far side of complexity."

How many people do you know—and work with—who either don't understand what Holmes was saying or suspect he was under the influence when he said it?

Unfortunately, these folks are all around us.

And their numbers appear to be increasing.

The media, particularly, condition us to want the quick and easy fix. We prefer a simplistic explanation rather than struggle with the complexities of personal and societal issues.

"Cut to the chase," people yell.

"Give us a quick fix," folks bellow.

"I don't have time for this," is the strident, constant shout.

We are rapidly adopting a short-cut mentality that prizes the urgent over the meaningful. "Doing *something*," seems more important than asking whether it needs doing at all. The faster we run to stay on top of daily crises and exigencies, the faster we distance ourselves from what's truly significant in our lives. What happens to be in front of us at the moment determines our priorities.

Are you getting the picture, leaders? You need to recognize the quick fix mentality and then help people deal with it in better ways.

You see, I think folks are increasingly losing control of their lives and their time, and don't know it. Things are in the saddle, Busyness is the new god. Band-aid approaches beat working on prevention; aspirins dull the pain that persists each day because of malignant internal elements. The long-term view of what's good for us is beyond our recognition abilities.

Your task, leaders, when your followers are examining problems and challenges, is to elevate the necessity of engaging in critical thinking rather than letting them settle for superficial answers. Help folks understand there is a need to take the time and expend the energy to think through and analyze complex issues. One simply can't hurry through everything!

Teach them, leaders, how to cope with complexity. Help them understand the dangers of simplification. Challenge them to develop critical thinking skills. Restore their faith in their abilities to think through matters on their own.

Too many people have become hustlers—too busy doing to learn how to evaluate what they're doing and why they're doing it.

I hope—like me—you've never met a hustler you've wanted to emulate.

Thoughts on Leadership

Leaders, here are a few comments about behavior that you may want to think about, then file away for future review:

When we recall our personal histories, we all become revisionists. We select what to remember, shape memories to fit positive self-perceptions, evaluate events in our favor, and put inflated spins on our accomplishments. We do much of this unconsciously, of course, but the purpose is clear—to reassure ourselves that we have not wasted our lives.

Wanting to believe something that enhances your self-perception usually distorts or weakens at least one fact.

Successful self-delusion provides the courage to try to deceive others.

A rigid attitude is an effort to hide insecurity or doubt, and sometimes both.

Repression is often an acceptable coping mechanism. It's okay to bury much of your thoughts and behavior. It does you no good to keep most of your transgressions and foolish actions on the surface of consciousness. However, selectivity is critical. Bury too many truths about yourself, and you impair opportunities for growth-correcting behaviors.

A Leader's Gift

Some people—and some leaders—have a special gift.

They enable you to accept and appreciate their criticism.

Others can make you defensive just by opening their mouths. You know you're not going to like what they say or the way they say it.

I suspect all of us are familiar with both kinds of people—and both kinds of criticism.

I remember an elementary school teacher who wasn't, I now believe, innately mean, yet her criticisms hurt every student in her class. She had a way of personalizing her comments in a manner that cut into the fragile shield that all children create to protect themselves from real and imagined fears.

There was also a teacher whose love and instinctual kindness encouraged us to become better students than we thought possible. She literally brought out the best in us. We interpreted her criticisms of our work as positive strokes of support from a person we *knew* cared deeply about each one of us.

No doubt you have formulated personal interpretations of criticism based on your unique experiences.

Here are a few thoughts regarding positive criticism I believe leaders should understand and prioritize above all others:

> ◇ When offering criticism, attack the problem, not the person. In my opinion, the best approach is, *"I have a problem and I need your help. My problem is that you seem unwilling to complete your responsibilities within the time limits we established."* This

places the problem on *your* shoulders, and you are asking for help. Few people will refuse to help you solve your problem. The worst approach is, *"You did it again, didn't you! You screwed it up again, just like I knew you would."* Your attack only makes the person defensive.

◇ Understand there is no such thing as negative criticism unless the person offering it is trying to be hurtful. The recipient of the criticism feels victimized. This is a sure indication that the criticism is hurtful rather than helpful.

◇ The most helpful criticism occurs when the person receiving it feels positive about it and gains insight from it. This is likely to come from a kind, respectful leader who is dedicated to helping the receiver understand how to close the distance between intentions, actions, and accomplishments. The best leaders care enough to provide hope and encouragement that the individual can do better, while offering motivation to try.

Shaw and Expectations

Let's think for a few moments about expectations.

Where better to begin than with George Bernard Shaw who wrote a play called *Pygmalion* from which the musical *My Fair Lady* was adapted.

There is one particular scene in the play that has serious implications for leaders. It's where Eliza Doolittle says to Colonel Pickering:

> *You see, apart from the things anyone can pick up (dressing, the proper way of speaking, etc.) the difference between a lady and a flower girl is not how she behaves but how she is treated. I shall always be a flower girl to Professor Higgins because he always treats me as a flower girl and always will. But I know I can be a lady to you because you always treat me as a lady and always will.*

What a clear and eloquent exposition of a self-fulfilling prophecy! Here's another example from the book *Pygmalion in the Classroom* about a fascinating experiment involving an intelligence test. Public school teachers were told about a test that would enable them to identify "late bloomers"—children who would have a sudden intellectual growth even though their IQs were now average or lower.

These youngsters were identified to the teachers, who were asked not to tell them or their parents about the test result, or to spend any additional time with them, or treat them differently in any other way.

When the children were retested a year later, their IQ scores had risen by thirty to forty percent in many cases. The teachers, of course, had been deceived; there was no test that measured late bloomers, and the children had been chosen at random.

So, what we expect from youngsters is what we're likely to get.

And that principle holds just as true for leaders. What a leader expects from followers is what he or she is likely to get as well.

When a leader establishes high standards for a project or sets goals that challenge people to achieve more than they thought possible, the chances are good that their participation activities will meet those high expectations.

The maxim for leaders? Expect much and you shall likely receive much in return.

Thoughts on Leadership

No matter how effective a leader becomes, she will experience set-backs from time to time. Look on the positive side. Disappointments can lead to growth and education if personal learning is the focus. Besides, a possible outcome of failure is humility—a precious and delicate quality that every good leader needs.

An effective leader should hold most convictions tentatively and accumulate them cautiously. Stubbornness and obstinacy about beliefs and opinions are not admirable qualities. A wise leader places a higher priority on questions and doubts than certainty.

One sign of leader maturity is when you realize that what people think of you no longer governs your behavior. The quality of your leadership abilities is more important. A second sign of maturity is recognizing that you are no longer susceptible to flattery and can distinguish it from sincere praise. And a third is realizing that no matter how successful you are as a leader, your self-importance is probably exaggerated.

How often a leader influences others and how unaware most leaders are when they do. Conversely, leaders are usually unaware how often others influence them. There is a frequency and naturalness about the process that escapes conscious detection. When someone says, "We're all in this together," this is usually what they mean.

For a leader, having blind faith is foolish. If faith is real, a leader's eyes should be open in order to discover the many exciting manifestations of a vision.

Hope and Idealism

What all effective leaders possess is hope. It's also what they share generously with others.

But how does a leader maintain hope in a world such as this?

Which is another way of asking how does a leader hold on to his or her idealism?

There's little doubt leaders face a constant struggle to maintain their idealism. I suspect effective leaders have considerable respect for Arthur Schlesinger's statement: "I am a short-term pessimist but a long-term optimist."

I know I do!

I was born in the Great Depression, was distantly exposed to the horrors of World War II when I was a youngster, served in the army in Korea in the early 1950s, grew to adulthood during the Cold War, was active in the civil rights movement during the sixties, and have lived to see the collapse of communism.

Like the rest of my generation I have seen human beings at their worst and at their best. Each day I read headlines that make me despair for the human race. Yet I try to imagine a more perfect world, just as I did when I was a child.

I believe this is the challenge leaders face daily. It's the noble, dedicated effort to keep hope alive despite dispiriting evidence of human frailty.

All leaders hold certain ideals that impact their judgment and decisions. They guide these ideals through life. While some leaders favor power or social status or the accumulation of honors, the best leaders choose the ideals of goodness, truth, and servanthood.

I have an inherent trust of leaders who have demonstrated a passionate interest in and a commitment to social justice and social responsibility. I admire leaders who have actively fought the evils of prejudice and discrimination against minorities and who champion by their deeds the ideals of universal brotherhood and sisterhood.

I especially admire leaders who share with others the hopefulness of idealism. They understand that without idealism the twin despairs of hopelessness and helplessness are free to take over individual lives. They know that idealism has the power to provide people with an optimistic view of the world. It enables folks to look for the positives within their lives and the lives of others.

I believe leaders choose to be idealists because they don't wish to be bound by present problems and troubles. They prefer to hope for a better world.

Thoughts on Leadership

One test of character for leaders is how they handle things they do not want to do.

A leader should attempt to identify and deal constructively with the darkness within his life. It's there, within all of us and is likely to get bigger unless dealt with constructively. It may take the form of prejudice, hatred, meanness, jealousy, indifference, greed, or selfishness. Or, the dark side could emerge as anger and envy as when someone else is honored for an achievement that we sought and thought we deserved.

Never play on people's fears, leaders. If you do, most individuals will know that you do not have their best interests at heart, and that you probably want something from them.

Humility and intolerance rarely coexist. The humble usually lack the arrogance that leads to exclusion and intolerance.

An extremist cannot be a successful leader unless followers believe in easy answers, simplistic solutions, absolute truths, and buy into the premise that the leader is entitled to hide those parts of self that would reveal embarrassing character weaknesses and illogical suppositions. Followers must also accept the principle that the leader is infallible in matters of doctrine and beliefs. Fanaticism and zealotry are the preferred methods of advancing their goals.

Still "Lerning"

Yes, yes, I know it's misspelled, but I'm trying to make a point.

And if you keep reading, you'll get it.

First of all, have you ever met this kind of person: "What I learn must conform with what I already know. Otherwise, it's not worth learning."

I presume that sounds to you like a statement by someone who has learned all he wants to know about the world. His mind is set—in concrete! New ideas, conflicting opinions, opposing beliefs are rejected, if indeed, considered at all.

Compare his attitude with a quote from the journalist, Bill Moyers: "When I learn something new—and it happens every day—I feel a little more at home in the universe, a little more comfortable in the nest. I'm afraid by the time I begin to feel really at home, it'll be over."

The first man probably believes that when he finished his formal schooling, his education was over. For him, graduation was a rite of passage; when he graduated he was no longer a child. I can hear him now. "Education is for young people. I was forced to go to school and coerced to learn. Why would I want to continue my education?"

How come some folks dislike learning so much and others, like Moyers, find it so exciting?

Did Moyers have a predisposition to learning? Was it family influence? Ambitious peers who became role models and motivated him to do better?

Whatever the reasons, Moyers realizes he has a lot to learn.

That's the attitude an effective leader must have—at least according to me, and I assume, Moyers.

However, we all know there are many leaders out there who are dispensing Truths and Absolutes, telling folks what they should believe and how they should think. These leaders are convinced they know what's right. Anyone who dissents is wrong. To them, educational systems that focus on questions rather than answers only confuse young minds.

So, in this context, there are two kind of leaders: one whose education is over and whose mind is closed. Then there's the other, who's excited by new learning and who sees the future as an open book.

One leader is satisfied with what he's "lerned;" the other isn't. Plus, he knows that an effective leader is always a student of leadership—he never knows enough!

Being Real

"Tom, do you recall the conversation we once had about the book, *The Velveteen Rabbit?*"

"Yes, what about it?"

"Remember when the rabbit asked the skin horse, 'What is real?' Well, that's what I want to ask you. Sometimes I become very confused and am not always sure what is real and what isn't. I'm often perplexed about whether I'm real."

"Do you recall the skin horse's answer? 'Real isn't how you are made. It's a thing that happens to you.' Then the horse added, 'It doesn't happen all at once. You become. It takes a long, long time.'"

"OK, Tom, so?"

"Well, *being* real is the first and most critical step to understanding *what* is real and what isn't. If you aren't authentic within your own identity then you will likely treat others in inconsistent ways."

"I can see that."

"Being real means thinking and behaving with integrity. You demonstrate inner coherence, soundness in judgment and honesty in your interactions with people."

"This is helpful. Please go on."

"Perhaps the most important aspect of a person's realness is coping with life's crises, as well as day-to-day problems, without relying on rationalizations."

"Say what?"

"In my opinion, one of the key ways we retain our mental health is by learning how to manage our present behavior without attempting to justify our past behavior. Instead of dealing with the present by using denial, compensation, rationalization, regression, or any of the other common defense mechanisms, we accept what is real and cope with it."

"That's not always easy."

"No, it isn't. A businessman deals with the reality of the bottom-line. A politician deals with votes; a scientist with facts; a poet, with feelings; a philosopher, with truth. Each of us responds to reality in our own way, depending on our interests, beliefs, and conditioning."

"So, to the philosopher, truth is what's most real, just as profit may define reality for the businessman?"

"Exactly. But there's a catch. Defining reality in terms of our primary role often leads to problems. The bottom-line mentality of a businessman will likely cause him problems at home if he attempts to transfer a bottom-line priority there. A scientist who wants only to deal with facts may have difficulty relating to his children."

"So, what are you saying?"

"That a person should define reality primarily by who he is. Being real begins with becoming an authentic person, not someone defined by job or vocation. While an individual who defines himself by work or other primary role often brings inconsistency to personal relationships and situations, a real person brings integrity to all he does."

"So, in terms of being real, who one is more important than what one does."

"Bingo!"

Thoughts on Leadership

Are you acquainted with the concept of "civitas," leaders? It means making sacrifices for the public good. Read Charles Sykes book, *A Nation of Victims*, for more insights and exposition of the term.

Leaders, it is more important that you bring honor to your position than rely on the position to reflect honor on you. Besides, that's the approach that garners the respect of others. A good leader impresses people through his abilities, not his position; he relates to people primarily through his qualities as a leader than through the office he holds.

An effective leader will want to hear all points of view on complex issues, but this approach doesn't mean that, after hearing them, she should treat all as having equal value.

◇◇◇

One mark of a mature leader is lack of a need to appear self-important.

◇◇◇

Every leader needs to feel affirmed. But most learn that praise from a person they respect is worth more than applause from the multitude.

◇◇◇

Never underestimate the value of timing in influencing the decision-making process. High quality knowledge, experience and information are next to useless if presented to a group or organization at the wrong time.

Taking Stock

An educator hired a ferryman to take him across a very large river. Once they were aboard the small boat, the passenger asked if the trip would be rough.

"Don't ask me nothin' about it," replied the ferryman.

"Have you ever studied grammar?" inquired the pedagogue.

"No."

"Then half your life is wasted!"

A short time later the river grew very rough, and the boat sprang a leak. The educator became agitated and asked what was wrong.

"Have you ever learned to swim?" asked the ferryman.

"No."

"Then your whole life is wasted because we're sinking."

What matters is often a matter of perspective, isn't it?

Many of us go through our life believing that what we do is important. And it may be—to us and those around us.

Somewhere along the line, however, we are likely to discover that what we know and what we do—and what we have done—are not significant in the large scheme of things.

We begin reflecting about our lives, priorities, ambitions, and the choices we have made.

We may decide that the directions we chose to pursue when young do not, from the perspective of experience and maturity, look as rosy and rewarding as they did earlier; that maybe some changes are in order.

Which is why we ought to think about taking stock of our lives every five years or so. How we choose to do this is less important than doing it.

It's also why I carried around for several decades the following poem by Natasha Josefowitz. Perhaps you'll appreciate why it has been so important to me.

I have not seen the plays in town only the computer printouts
I have not read the latest books only the Wall Street Journal
I have not heard the birds sing this year only the sound of typewriters
I have not taken a walk anywhere but from the parking lot to my office
I have not shared a feeling in years but my thoughts are known to all
I have not shed a tear in ages but when I shout they tremble
I have not listened to my own needs but what I want I get
I have arrived—but is this where I was going?

Leaders, it's difficult to help others get where they're going if you don't know where you're going.

Be Yourself

"Be yourself!"

How often have you heard this advice? Or given it?

"Oh, you can handle that problem if you just be yourself."

"You won't get into trouble if you just be yourself."

The fact is that's the worst advice you can give some folks.

Obviously you wouldn't offer this counsel to a rapist, murderer, embezzler or child abuser.

Nor would you want to direct this gem toward a neurotic or hypochondriac.

And maybe you wouldn't choose to share it with a stressed-out executive, religious zealot, bully, town gossip or closet boozer.

There are probably many people we would prefer not to be themselves.

Of course, I realize we often give this advice when we mean the recipient should simply be honest with himself and others. "Just say what you mean," is our counsel.

But this assumes the person is capable of honesty and understands intent. Which frequently isn't the case. After all, each of us has a considerable gift for self-deception and a large reservoir of internal disorder, resulting in inability to either express ourselves honestly or state accurately what we mean. We speak and act repeatedly out of self-confusion and bewilderment.

In a real sense, we may be deficient of adequate information about ourselves. We lack self-knowledge. We are ignorant about what we think, what we believe, what our values are—in short, who we are. Telling this kind of person to "be yourself" is less than helpful; it's personally threatening. She doesn't know who her "self" is, thus is fearful that whatever decision she makes or action she initiates will be wrong or make her look foolish. Lacking an understanding of self produces fear of making decisions or taking action.

As Will Rogers once said, "Everybody is ignorant, only on different subjects." But we need not be ignorant about ourselves. To a large degree, self-knowledge is the key to living a fulfilling life.

And self-knowledge is critical for leaders. It enables you to know what your strengths and limitations are, to use your skills and knowledge to lead others, to know when to be quiet, when to engage others in discussions, and when to be active, to relate to different individuals and to understand what needs to be learned in order to be a better person and better leader.

With regard to understanding self, the goal of a leader is to be able to respond positively to the admonition "Be yourself" with the words, "Okay, I pretty well know who I am. I can do that!"

Healthy Leaders—Healthy Organizations

Healthy leaders and healthy organizations; more often than not, they **are** connected.

Let's look at them separately and examine the parallels.

No doubt we can agree that an effective leader is a mentally-healthy individual. But, how do we define mental health? Looking at the literature, it's been defined in a number of ways: the ability to fulfill one's social function, to carry out a job in a productive manner, or to reproduce oneself. It has also been defined as adjustment to life's daily tensions, cooperativeness, or tolerance for other individuals and their differences. It's been described in terms of feeling secure in interpersonal interactions. Some call mental health the absence of mental illness—the ability to "get along or go along." A stress-related definition indicates that one is mentally healthy if the individual knows when to fight, knows when to take flight, or when neither response works, when to *flow.*

Dr. Karl Menninger, in his book, *The Human Mind,* gave us this definition:

> *Let us define mental health as the adjustment of human beings to the world and to each other with a maximum of effectiveness and happiness. Not just efficiency, or just contentment—or the grace of obeying the rules of the game cheerfully. It is all of these together. It is the ability to maintain an even temper, an alert intelligence, socially considerate behavior, and a happy disposition. This, I think, is a healthy mind.*

Almost four decades ago at The Menninger Foundation, two staff persons (Drs. Solley and Munden) became interested in defining mental health. They asked fourteen senior clinicians to describe five persons they considered to be mentally solid individuals. Approximately eighty people were described. The two researchers then sought to find common characteristics which, they concluded, would identify mentally healthy individuals. What are these common characteristics?

First, mentally healthy people treat other folks as individuals without categorizing them. They are able to see the uniqueness of each person and open themselves to the rich variety that different people have to offer.

Second, they find gratification in a variety of sources. All of their psychological needs aren't in one basket. They have a number of ways of enjoying themselves, of having fun, of getting satisfaction.

Third, they are flexible under stress. They cope with problems in a number of different ways. When one method of solving a problem doesn't work, they try another tack. They adopt strategies that enable them to find alternative solutions to problems.

Fourth, mentally healthy people identify their strengths and accept their limitations. They neither depreciate nor over-value their abilities and talents.

And last, they are qualitatively active and productive. They are active because they enjoy what they are doing while their productive activities afford them pleasure.

At this point, it's important to understand that the state of mental health is not a static condition. Rather, an individual is always in the process of becoming mentally healthy as opposed to being there or, in reverse, in the process of becoming mentally unhealthy. Mental health is a continuous, progressive actualization of values that makes life worth living despite the miseries that exact their inevitable toll on us. As a matter of fact, it's through suffering and temporary defeats that we learn to deal constructively and positively with the complex realities of our lives.

Perhaps the best description of mental illness is this: *it occurs when a person attempts to avoid suffering.* That's when an individual begins self-medicating and gets into trouble. Suffering is part of living, just as joy is. It goes with the territory. It's how a person handles suffering that largely determines how mentally healthy the individual will be.

Need help in improving your mental health? Dr. Menninger provided us with several guidelines leaders might wish to think about:

- ◇ Set up as an ideal the facing of reality as honestly and as cheerfully as possible.

- ◇ Cultivate social contacts and cultural developments.

- ◇ Recognize neurotic evasions as such and take advantage of opportunities for sublimation. (Substitute hobbies for habits.)

- ◇ Learn to know the evidences of mental pathology and how best to deal with them.

- ◇ Assume that the unhappy are always (at least partly) wrong.

Now, leaders, let's turn our attention to the criteria that characterize healthy organizations. The following checklist of interrelated characteristics describes organizations that nurture mentally healthy employees by fostering mentally healthy environments.

It may be obvious, but it needs to be said that leaders who are mentally healthy themselves have a far better chance of influencing, producing, and maintaining healthy environments than leaders with poor mental health. There is a contagious element between leaders and followers.

1. In a healthy organization, *appreciation of people and concern for their well-being* is the most important value leaders can hold. In a seminal study undertaken in 1986 by the U.S. Chamber of Commerce, ten items of "worker desire" as ranked by employees were compared against the same ten items as ranked by what employers thought their employees wanted. The results are staggering. The top three *highest* values for employees—appreciation, feeling "in" on things, and help with personal problems—were the three *lowest* values employers assumed desirable to employees.

   Employers thought that money, job security, and upward mobility were the highest priorities for employees. The fact that workers ranked relationships ahead of wages and promotions should be of major consequence to leaders of organizations. Healthy organizations focus on this as a priority.

2. The organization is *productive.* If it is a for-profit organization, it makes a profit. If not for-profit, it measures productivity in other ways. When a company operates at a break-even margin or at a loss, or any organization fails in its measure of productivity, not only will it take on an unhealthy pallor, but the employees will evidence signs of distress. A healthy organization is driven by productive, quality work, not by busy work or out of a sense of desperation. People who feel their work matters derive pleasure and a sense of worth that is basic to elevating their self-esteem.

   The best organizations have a collaborative approach to work as opposed to a competitive approach. There is a shared mission and employees feel they are integral contributors to achieving success. Consequently, they are motivated to give the organization their best efforts.

3. A healthy organization *accepts its strengths and limitations.* Consulting with employees at varying levels of the organization, leaders chart a course that recognizes what the organization

can do and cannot do, where and when to expand, and when to put the brakes on. There is a clear understanding throughout the organization of major goals and purposes, and these are well-developed and communicated so that all employees understand them.

The organization builds on its attributes but doesn't overvalue, just as it doesn't depreciate itself. There is a commitment to either accepting limitations that cannot, and perhaps should not be changed, or decreasing those limitations.

4. A healthy organization *deals constructively with reality.* There is a strong commitment to honesty that permeates the organization at all levels. Its leaders believe that telling the truth—and encouraging employees throughout the organization to speak the truth—is a high and critical priority.

    When dealing with difficult and complex issues, a positive attitude envelopes the project, but not in a "rose-colored," tainted way. Rather, the approach is to identify problems, then move to find the best ways of dealing with them in order to reach resolutions. "Group-think" is avoided as are other defensive processes. When conflict occurs between employees or groups, it's handled openly and constructively. Indeed, the organization encourages the airing and resolving of conflict, recognizing that growth, learning and improvements will emerge through the conflict of ideas, opinions, and viewpoints. There is a clear understanding that the more constructively conflict is handled, the more mature that organization is in its interpersonal relationships.

5. A healthy organization *adapts to change,* the one constant it faces each day. There is a recognition that daily changes will occur, they must be handled, and the more positive the attitude toward those changes, the more likely are they to be dealt with constructively.

Insofar as possible, leaders anticipate changes by establishing an active, continuing antenna system through participating in planning sessions, reading pertinent publications, assessing data projections, and listening to employees at different levels of the organization. In addition, leaders study the dynamics of change and ensure that key individuals become versed on the psychological impact of change through discussions, readings, and formal training sessions.

In coping with change, leaders know that the more adaptable they are, the more adaptable their employees and the organization will likely be. In times of rapid change, adaptability is not only a requisite for survival but a necessity for productive growth.

6. A healthy organization fosters an environment through its policies, procedures, and practices that enable employees to feel they are *treated in a consistent manner.* While an organization is compelled to respond to differing pressures and needs in accordance with its mission, it strives for consistency in its approach to employees. For one thing, it doesn't categorize folks by treating one group—based on age, race, gender, ethnicity or sexual orientation—differently than others. Rather, each person is treated as unique; the individual's personality and personal skills and knowledge are what sets him or her apart.

Leaders communicate their appreciation of employees in a number of ways that make them feel they are valuable, contributing members of the organization regardless of their position.

Although no organization will ever achieve a perfect record of internal consistency, it's the commitment to achieving a high level that contributes to the integrity of that organization. Integrity can be evaluated by two basic criteria: the consistency of its treatment of employees, and the consistency of what it says it does compared with what it actually delivers. In other words, it's commitment to truth.

7. Another characteristic of a healthy organization is that its employees are *relatively free from distress.* As indicated in the section, "Leaders and Stress," stress is part of life and part of all jobs; distress need not be. Distress causes suffering and pain, and contributes to physical and psychological illness.

    Distress occurs when any number of conditions are present:

    ◇ When leaders fail to show appreciation for the efforts of their employees and do not communicate that they care about them as human beings

    ◇ When employees are not made to feel they are important to the organization

    ◇ When leaders are out of touch with the needs and values of employees

    ◇ When leaders separate themselves, by word and deed, from employees

    ◇ When discrimination is allowed to exist within the organization

    ◇ When rewards are not reasonably commensurate with tasks performed

    ◇ When management is crisis-oriented

    ◇ When employees are treated inconsistently

    ◇ When employees have no control over their specific work responsibilities

    ◇ When organizational politics determine job advancement

    As every leader knows, this is by no means a complete list of conditions that foster distress. The point is, healthy organizations work hard to nurture conditions that prevent distress from occurring. They encourage employees at all levels to actively communicate with leaders in a participative manner that not only prevents negative conditions from developing, but works continually to see that healthy conditions are maintained.

8. A healthy organization provides employees with opportunities for *diverse gratifications*. Multiple challenges and assignments provoke not only continuous job challenges but differing interpersonal relationships as well.

   People are motivated when they are given responsibility and opportunities to achieve; when they feel their efforts are recognized; when they have chances for personal growth; and when the work itself is rewarding. Leaders in healthy organizations recognize the challenge of activating each individual with different incentives at different times.

9. Within a healthy organization there is a *pervasive enthusiasm*. Smiles and laughter are far more common than frowns and bitching. Work is accomplished not because employees feel they have to, but because they want to. There is a strong sense of loyalty at all levels. It's this loyalty and enthusiasm that provides employees with the desire to want to make a positive contribution each day.

10. Coupled with the above is the reality that a healthy organization nurtures an environment that cultivates a *sense of humor*. Employees work hard but have fun in the process. They play well during free time and work well during work time. They understand they need to be serious in their work performance, but try not to take themselves too seriously. Leaders exhibit the same attitude. Employees can laugh at themselves, at their irrationality, and it's tolerated throughout the organization. A healthy organization communicates the perspective that life goes on no matter what—and that life should be filled with the contagious joy of humor.

11. Finally, a healthy organization *cares*. Each employee feels the organization cares about her or him as an individual. Leaders evidence their care in a number of ways, e.g., remembering names, birthdays, anniversaries, and special events; inquiring sincerely about employee's welfare, and about their work and professional lives; calling and visiting during illnesses.

When leaders do these things, employees tend to reciprocate which, of course, extends the spirit of caring. When shared internally, it's easy to extend the caring attitude to clients, families, and friends. Perhaps this highly contagious spirit of caring is the truly necessary requisite for a healthy organization. Without it, leaders would have a tough time supporting the other ten.

Thoughts on Leadership

Effective leaders have a sense of the unknowable and an ability to foresee the unforeseeable.

Leaders can be evaluated on how well they have communicated to followers the message that each of them is responsible for the welfare of the entity they are serving. The objective is to have all those involved feel their efforts and caring make a difference.

A public servant should regard his position as ad hoc. Otherwise he may try to become a long-term inhabitant of a leadership position in which the lust for power takes precedence over the servant function.

Strong, ethical leaders are at a premium. The public deserves individuals whose moral leadership raises the consciousness, values and standards of its citizens.

Leadership is developed. Ordinary folks can become leaders if they are willing to commit time and energy to maximizing their leadership abilities along with learning certain leadership skills.

Effective leaders possess confidence and self-esteem. They have a history of challenging difficult tasks and handling them successfully as well as learning from their mistakes. They have the capacity to recover from harsh, negative experiences and move on.

The best leaders have experience as good followers.

A Mayor and the River

Once upon a time in a town surrounded by the forest, a mayor pondered the deterioration of his community which had thrived under his predecessor.

He decided to seek the counsel of a former mayor whom he respected and admired.

After explaining the situation to her, he waited eagerly for her response. But she said not a word. Rather, she gestured for him to follow her.

Silently they walked several miles to a wide river. After sitting quietly for several hours looking intently at the river, the former mayor began gathering wood, then built a large fire. When the flames were aglow, she bid him to sit by her side. There they sat for hours as the fire burned brightly into the night.

When dawn was breaking and the flames were small and weak, she finally spoke to him. "Do you now understand why you are unable to sustain the greatness of our community as your predecessor did?"

Greatly perplexed, he was ashamed that he could not answer the old lady's question. "I'm sorry, but I don't understand what you are getting at."

With patience and a smile the former mayor spoke for a second time. "Reflect, for a few minutes, on the fire that burned so brightly before us last night. How strong and powerful it was. No huge trees or great beasts could have matched its mighty force. It possessed the power to conquer all that lay in its path.

"Consider also the river. It begins as a small stream, then flows slowly downward permeating every crack and seeking out every crevice in its journey to the sea. When we listen to the water, it can scarcely be heard. When we touch it, it can hardly be felt, so gentle is its nature.

"Yet, look now at the once mighty fire. All that remains are ashes. You see, the fire is so strong that it destroys all that lies in its path but it eventually falls prey to its own strength and is consumed. Not so with the calm and quiet river. It flows on, growing deeper and broader and more powerful, providing life and sustenance to all.

"This is the lesson for a leader such as you. It is not the fire, but the water that is the well of life. It is not mighty and authoritative leaders but leaders who are humble and possess deep inner strength who capture people's hearts and nurture the lives of those around them. Good fortune is not sustained in a sudden flame, but in a quiet consistency that moves each day in one direction.

"You need to reflect on the type of leader you are. Perhaps the answer you seek rests there."

Suddenly the mayor understood what his old friend was saying. No longer puzzled, he looked into her eyes with an enlightened smile. Then he turned toward the river. He saw it differently than he had last night. Nor would it ever appear the same to him again.

(Adapted from an Oriental parable)

Thoughts on Leadership

A major challenge facing a public servant is to reconcile the needs of the general public with the self-interests of vocal citizens.

Leaders will inevitably encounter the wrath of mean-spirited individuals. One reason some folks are mean is they have little to look back on with pride and even less to look forward to with hope. Their anger is often directed at leaders as their way of getting even for the kind of unsuccessful life they have led. Envy is, of course, at the root of their anger and mean-spiritedness.

One of the toughest challenges for a sensible leader is to try to make sense of an argument when debating with a colleague who lacks sensibility.

Effective leaders understand that although creative individuals have the ability to energize and inspire groups, they also may be regarded as troublemakers because they frequently challenge the status quo. Leaders need to find the means to encourage these inventive, resourceful individuals and even protect them when necessary without alienating others. Help colleagues and associates understand that creativity is like a flower—praise and attention make it bloom, indifference or discouragement nips it in the bud. Appreciation is to a new or fresh idea what water is to a plant.

Leaders, try to rise above any position you hold in an organization. Work to define the position; don't let the position define you. People you work with should have a higher regard for your personal and professional qualities than for the office you hold. Remember that self-respect gains respect; self-importance diminishes respect.

The Elusive Big B

So few of us have it.

Even too few leaders possess it.

When it's within our grasp, it skitters away.

When we court it, it turns seductive.

If we set it as a goal, we define and redefine it repeatedly.

When we seize one part of it, the other components often slide away.

If we manage to function smoothly with two parts of it, the third and fourth parts become more frustratingly elusive.

In our early years we don't recognize it's even an issue.

In our adolescent years, with too many problems to distract us, it seldom enters our consciousness.

As young adults, we get occasional glimpses of it, but building a career and starting a family are higher priorities.

In the middle years, it gets periodic lip service but infrequent attention. We begin to understand it's important, but have yet formed no clear internal diagram of how to make it a meaningful part of our lives.

For most of us, by the time we recognize how important the four parts are, we've forfeited our ability to pull them together with ease.

What is it?

It's **balance**.

It's the harmony of our intelligence, our physical selves, our emotional being, and our spiritual consciousness that become the whole entity called "Me!"

What all of us need to understand—especially leaders—is that when we neglect developing any part of ourselves, we pay for it one way or another.

We risk losing the ability to appreciate whatever part of the world we are denying or avoiding.

If we fail to develop our intelligence, we decline in our ability to comprehend the changing world in which we live.

If we neglect the physical part of our self, our body sends urgent messages until the abuse overwhelms them.

If we disregard the emotional side, we lose the ability to see the rich colors and hear the magnificent music that enriches our world.

And if we ignore the spiritual side, we confine ourselves to self-imposed walls that hide the soul from the real treasures of the world that lie just beyond our temporal understanding.

It's possible that true wisdom comes only to those who have achieved a reasonable blending of these four elements.

It is also possible that a major part of wisdom is recognizing that a perfect combination is impossible, and that the challenge of life is to work toward putting these four critical components of self into balance.

Part of wisdom provides the opportunity to demonstrate to those of the younger generation who are struggling with the daily, forceful exigencies of studying or making a living, that they will be able to achieve a balance only if they begin practicing it early.

While parents and older friends can make a difference in the lives of younger people by conveying to them the value of working toward balance in their lives, the influence of leaders in this regard cannot be underestimated. Teachers, scout leaders, coaches and other adults who serve and lead youth have a significant impact on the development of young folks. Encouraging them to seek balance as they approach adulthood should be an important part of their growth and development.

Advice? Avoid It

Leaders—want some advice?

Don't take any. It could be dangerous to your health.

It seems almost un–American to denounce advice, but that's what I'm doing. Let me identify the advice I'm railing against. It's the kind that begins with the words, "Let me tell you what you should do." Or, "If I were you, here's what I would do." Or, "Here's the way to do it." Get the picture?

To illustrate the problem, listen to the great philosopher, Charlie Brown. In a four-picture cartoon series which appeared years ago, CB is on the mound preparing to throw a pitch. In the first frame Linus, the catcher, calls for a fast ball. In the next frame CB is told by Lucy to throw a curve. In the third, he is surrounded by the entire team, each exhorting him to throw a different pitch. Finally, CB is standing alone on the mound and he utters this touching, plaintive statement: "This world is filled with people anxious to function in an advisory capacity."

Indeed it is, Charlie Brown.

"It works for me so it will work for you." Wrong! What works for me may not work for you. Each of us is unique and different. But let me tell you what I really have against giving advice. I give it, you take it, and it works. Now, I'm in trouble.

You see, if I give you advice three things can happen, and only one of them is good; you don't accept it. The other two possibilities are negatives. You take it and it works. Then you'll come back for more. This creates dependency which leads to anger. The second possibility is that it doesn't work. Then you'll complain about my bad advice. I lose either way.

I try hard never to give advice. If asked for my opinion, rather than advice, I attempt to give counsel—options, alternatives, choices. Advice tends to shift responsibility for the decision from *your* shoulders to mine. Presenting alternatives from which you can choose, leaves the responsibility where it belongs—on *your* shoulders.

I have enough of a problem making good decisions about my life; no way do I feel confident (or arrogant) enough to make decisions for you.

That wasn't always true for me. (Listen up, leaders; I suspect you can identify with this!) When I was young and inexperienced, I would tell my staff to call me anytime if they had a problem. "Don't hesitate to call me at home," I used to say. Guess what? They did. And they'd usually begin with, "Hello Ron, we've got a problem." It took me several months to catch on that when I gave them advice and we hung up the phone, I had the problem and they didn't! I was so eager to play the authority that I fell willingly into their trap.

I don't do that anymore. Now, if anyone calls and asks for advice, I provide counsel and leave the responsibility where it belongs—with the caller.

Thoughts on Leadership

Leaders, take everything to heart and your heart will likely wear out sooner than it should.

When facing major decisions, be sure to give your heart a fair hearing. It always has your best interest at stake.

One mark of a wise leader is to seek the counsel of others with some degree of regularity, knowing you cannot have the answers to all questions.

Andre Gide said: "Everything that needs to be said has already been said, but since no one was listening, everything must be said again." With this realization comes the crashing need to endure and persevere. Accepting gracefully what you've seen or heard or experienced before requires, most of all, that you learn to put up with yourself.

Leaders need to know how to renew themselves. Whether it's a walk in the woods, attending a special class, working in the garden, or going for a bike ride, the activity should give your mind time to relax and your spirit a chance to recover.

Blessed Are Leaders Who...

Some leaders are blessed, some are not.

Some seem to have their act together to the degree that one wants either to emulate them or join up as a follower.

I have my own criteria about role-model leaders, just as you have.

Putting mine in the context of the Beatitudes, here are a few characteristics of leaders I admire.

Blessed are those who think before they talk, for they shall earn my everlasting gratitude.

Blessed are those who have the gift of sharing with me no more than I want to know, for they will surprise and please me.

Blessed are those who speak concisely, for they will become my chosen minority.

Blessed are those who listen proactively, for they shall receive the same respect from me.

Blessed are those who speak in small truths, for they will lead me to rethink what I think I know.

Blessed are those who don't hold me to words I express during a heated argument, for they have learned the meaning of forgiveness or have selective memories that deserve enshrinement.

Blessed are those who don't give me advice, for they know the difference between advice and counsel.

Blessed are those who don't label people, for they humanize our lives.

Blessed are those who can laugh at themselves, for their humor will be as contagious as their sense of self.

Blessed are those who know me and still love me, for they shall receive my love and admiration.

Blessed are those who will risk their friendship for me, for they are my true friends.

Blessed are those who identify with Don Quixote, for their dreams will give the rest of us hope.

Blessed are those who agree with Socrates that the unexamined life isn't worth living.

Blessed are those who have read this far, for they shall surely enter....

Dream, Leaders, Dream

"To dream the impossible dream."

Recognize the line?

It's from *Man of La Mancha,* that beautiful and powerful musical based on the writings of Miguel Cervantes.

The writer also had Don Quixote speak these words: "The truth of a man lies in his dreams."

Dreams! What would a person be without them?

Where would the world be without dreams?

Where would leaders be without dreams?

Bob Greenleaf assured us that great accomplishments are preceded by great dreams. That's worth thinking about, isn't it?

I believe the best leaders are motivated by their dreams! It's their dreams that provide hope and direction along with the motivation to achieve them. And the best leaders have the ability to translate those dreams into realities that carry the rest of us along with them.

Back in the early 70s I read two books by Dr. Hans Selye. (Remember, I referred to him earlier?) He wrote a few words I have appreciated more than, perhaps, any I have ever read. They have had considerable impact upon my life:

Realistic people who pursue practical aims, are rarely as realistic or practical, in the long run of life, as the dreamers who pursue their dreams.

233

Much of my life has been guided by dreams. I dreamed of changing the world; I decided during the fifth decade of life to be satisfied with simply influencing it in my own small way.

I dreamed of a nation where equal rights would be shared by all its citizens and that I would help that happen. I was active in the civil rights movement during the early 60s, but know how little I accomplished and how far we still have to go to achieve justice for all.

I dreamed in the early 70s of helping to design the first experimental city in the world—a city in Minnesota that would utilize cutting-edge technology and be an environmental leap forward that would enable present cities to learn from our efforts and exceed our dreams. My contribution would be to develop a Learning System. The experimental city was killed by the Minnesota Legislature because of economic realities.

I dreamed in the 80s about promoting societal change by helping business and governmental leaders understand how to utilize their strengths and gifts in ways that would not only make their personal lives more fulfilling, but more influential within society as well. I was only mildly successful in achieving that goal.

But, from those experiences, I certainly learned a lot about myself and about leaders, and about the significance of dreams.

And you know what? There's not one of those unfulfilled dreams I wouldn't pursue again if I had the opportunity—and the energy.

Having a great dream is better than not having one at all. Pursuing the dream and falling short is better than not taking a shot at it.

Some great dreams aren't going to be realized. But making the effort is what's important.

I believe good leaders pay attention not only to their dreams, but to the dreams of those folks with whom they associate. It's through our dreams, and the dreams of others, that we weave the tapestries that give meaning to our lives. Understand others' dreams and a leader can begin to grasp the issues which are important within their lives.

As an example, I think leaders should have a handle on the developmental stages people go through so they can understand the aging issues each of us struggles with.

Here's a brief and incomplete summary of what I mean.

The very young frequently use dreams as a primary way of coping with the awesome, confusing world they are confronting. To watch a child play is to see the fullest expression of a dream world become real.

For adolescents, dreams are a vehicle that enables them to break loose from the constant challenge of identity problems. It's dreams that permit them to confront a mirror and see beyond the acne, braces, and imperfect bodies.

A young adult dreams of success. "Watch me go, world! I shall be famous and respected!" Dreams motivate, even when daily hassles depress or disillusion.

Middle-aged adults dream about what might have been, until they realize that the real questions are, "What will I be? Will I be healthy, happy, loved in my later years? What have I achieved, and what is left for me?"

It's in the middle years that we confront youthful dreams and devise new ones.

Finally in the later years, a person's dreams turn outward. Looking back, around, and forward, dreams focus on loved ones, family, community, and again on the world. But now one dreams of leaving the world a little better place than it would have been without him or her.

It is perhaps in a person's later years that dreams attain a luster earlier ones cannot achieve. It's then that more people have time for reflection, time to ponder the larger questions of life. Dreams can provide meaning as they make daily life better.

Henry David Thoreau wrote: "If one advances confidently in the direction of his dreams, and endeavors to live the life which he has imagined, he will meet with a success unexpected in common hours."

Leaders, keep those dreams alive.

So you can be!

Thoughts on Leadership

One personal deficit or flaw can prevent a leader from achieving success. It may be inattention to details, lack of basic communication skills, poor temper control, inability to see the large picture, racial or gender bias, immoderate personal habits, or a self-centered approach to relationships. The key to success is to discover your limitations, either by self-analysis or through the assistance of friends or a therapist, then correct them.

One deficiency of some leaders is the tendency to move backward into the future. They hardly know where they're going until they get there. Whether due to a lack of vision or a preference for crisis management, they often ignore road maps and planning strategies, then choose the capricious route of hindsight and dumb luck.

Leaders, wound the self-esteem of a follower and you damage her will power. Will power requires self-esteem.

A relevant question for every leader is, "Am I a better leader today than I was a month or year ago?"

Leaders would do well to act on the premise that every person deserves the same respect and courtesy that we expect from them.

Tolstoy and Character

What makes a good person?

How can we raise children to be good people with strong moral characters and values that will guide and sustain them through life?

My experience has taught me that the best leaders are also good human beings. And they wouldn't be good at either if they hadn't been raised by parents and other caring adults in a manner that helped them develop positive character traits and values.

Yes, yes, there are specific leadership qualities and skills that one needs to be an effective leader over and above those that identify a good person, but a good man or woman can readily learn how to be a good leader.

It's the lessons a young person learns that are instrumental in preparing him or her to live a positive and constructive life as an adult. And the best lessons are often those that are conveyed to young folks through stories. Every child loves stories, of course. It's almost impossible to exaggerate their value.

Here's one of my favorites. It's by Leo Tolstoy.

> *The grandfather had become very old. His legs wouldn't go, his eyes didn't see, his ears didn't hear, he had no teeth. And when he ate, the food dripped from his mouth.*
>
> *The son and daughter-in-law stopped setting a place for him at the table and gave him supper in back of the stove. Once they brought dinner down to him in a cup. The old man wanted to move the cup and dropped and broke it. The daughter-in-law began to grumble at the old man for spoiling everything in the house and breaking the*

cups and said that she would now give him dinner in a dishpan. The old man only sighed and said nothing.

Once the husband and wife were staying home and watching their small son playing on the floor with some wooden planks. He was building something. The father asked, "What is that you are doing, Misha?" And Misha said, "Dear Father, I am making a dishpan, so that when you and dear Mother become old, you may be fed from this dishpan."

The husband and wife looked at one another and began to weep. They became ashamed of so offending the old man, and from then on seated him at the table and waited on him.

Think on this story, leaders. How many lessons can be learned from it! And what kind of a discussion might you provoke concerning moral values and qualities of character that need to be championed and developed.

Effective leaders will sometimes discover they are in the midst of teaching opportunities. Stories like this one are often good places to begin.

Lessons Leaders Learn

Leaders, have you ever considered how many significant lessons you've learned in your lifetime? Maybe you've even learned a few within these pages!

I learned more than I could handle before I started school, then at least hundreds during the many years I spent in classrooms, then hundreds, maybe thousands more after I left school. I suspect your story is similar.

Through the years each of us accumulates a sizable number—some of which we remember and cherish. The best ones we pass along to children and grandchildren and to others with whom we interact.

What follows are several more lessons I've learned that have implications for leaders. Hopefully, you'll resonate with them and perhaps feel impelled to add to the list lessons that have particular meaning for you.

- ◇ One of the most significant lessons involves the issue of **control.** Leaders know that there are folks out there with controlling personalities. First question: Are you one of them? If so, either start figuring out why you have a need to exert control over people and situations, or seek professional help. Until you get this problem under control, you will be less than an effective leader. Once you have it managed, you can turn your attention to helping those followers who want to control you and others.

- ◇ Your **intelligence** is no guarantee that you will be a good leader, just as your **sensitivity** doesn't necessarily mean you will be compassionate toward others. Purpose, intent and commitment come into these equations big time! An effective leader understands that compassion is more important in serving others than intelligence.

◇ Either be gifted with—or quickly develop—a **sense of humor**, or you'll soon find yourself leading a phantom coterie of followers. Leaders who can laugh at themselves will be admired and tolerated, even when they screw up in small ways. An effective leader knows when to use humor, how best to use it, and what to say that will cut through those inevitable, tedious discussions that are going nowhere. Fortunate is the leader who is appreciative of whimsy, irony, comedy, and buffoonery. And fortunate are his or her followers.

◇ Leaders, check out your **attitude**, and pay close attention to it. Why? Because the darn thing will change on you, sometimes when you least expect it. To lead a group, you know that the more positive you are, the more likely it is that your followers will receive positive vibes. But, there are times—as you are doubtless aware—when something negative will get to you and throw you into, or at least in the direction of, a funk. Be sensitive to those moments and then make the necessary correction.

◇ Effective leadership is always rooted in the innate **character** that resides within you and is exhibited before others. Your integrity—inner consistency—is what will encourage people to follow and admire you, not only as their leader but as a person. It takes time and considerable commitment to develop a character rooted in a goodness that is seen by others to be caring, loving, and truly concerned about their welfare. It may be the single most important quality a leader possess.

◇ It's important that leaders join what Marian Wright Edelman calls the Fellowship of Human Beings. The guiding principle calls for you to seek the **inclusion** of people different from you and to practice actively healing and love whenever possible.

Thoughts on Leadership

The dread of failure sometimes causes leaders to fear success.

A successful leader cannot be a surface thinker. An approach to responsibilities that accepts superficiality will likely lead to false and dangerous conclusions.

Leaders, if you're concerned about your image, you probably have a character problem. A person of integrity doesn't need to worry about the image she is projecting to others.

For a leader, self-satisfaction is the first stop on the road south.

An effective leader doesn't let the words "I don't care what people think," pass her lips. Not only should that statement disqualify her as a leader, but it's dishonest as well.

You've got your work cut out for you, leaders, when you are associated with someone who persists in telling you and others "the way it is," rather than the "way he sees it."

People who insist they are always "right" may not be fully human. To err is human!

The Hopes of Leaders

I was speaking a few months ago to a group of leaders about **hope**.

And then last week, I ran across a statement by Vaclav Havel: "Hope is…not the conviction that something will turn out well, but the certainty that something makes sense, regardless of how it turns out."

Like the rest of you I want the things I work for to turn out well. Unfortunately, hope doesn't necessarily follow my neat agenda, no matter how determined I am.

The fateful question many leaders struggle with is, "How do we know our positive actions make any difference at all?"

Havel's point is, of course, that we have no assurance they will. But our small efforts to make a positive difference makes sense regardless of the outcome.

Years ago when I was in graduate school at the University of Colorado, my Beloved and I taught a Sunday school class of youngsters who had just completed their junior high school years. We remained their teachers and involved in their lives until they graduated from high school. After several moves and a lapse of almost fifty years, we have lost contact with them. Naturally we wonder how they've turned out. Did we have any lasting influence on their lives?

We'll never know, but we do know that the experience of all those Sundays, all those private times we had together, and all those picnics and dances and roller skating parties we enjoyed as their friends and mentors had a significant impact upon our lives. We grew as individuals because of the love we shared with them.

Historian Arnold Toynbee spoke directly to this point: "The first hope in our inventory—the hope that includes and at the same time transcends all others—must be the hope that love is going to have the last word."

I can live with that. In befriending those precious youngsters we somehow understood that just showing up—just being there for them—over the course of those four years, while we tried to do the right thing and say the right words, would have a positive impact on their lives.

But perhaps as important, my Beloved and I accepted the challenge of using whatever talents and skills we possessed in order to become more than we ever expected to be. We achieved more from our relationships with those boys and girls than we ever thought possible. They made a positive difference in our lives, for sure.

"I have never felt anything really mattered but the satisfaction of knowing that you stood for the things in which you believed and had done the very best you could." Eleanor Roosevelt said that.

Hope may depend less on what we expect of others than on what we expect of ourselves. I can live with that too!

I hope leaders can as well.

Thoughts on Leadership

Every time leaders journey beyond the comfort and safety of their cognitive mind, they open themselves to mystery, challenge, and the consequences of being changed.

Leaders who have permitted themselves to be stripped of their sense of wonder aren't aware of how unappealing they may now appear to others.

One difference between a public servant and a politician is that a politician is sometimes unaware he is stumbling over the truth; a public servant knows and is determined not to make that mistake. Another difference is that the politician tends to base decisions primarily on the next election; the public servant on the next generation.

I have had the good fortune in my life of meeting three leaders who, I decided, were near-perfect servant-leaders. They, of course, disagreed.

One of the tests of a leader is how she handles individuals in a group whose absence would make her heart grow fonder.

Serving as a leader would be so much easier if experience taught one how to avoid the first mistake as well as the second.

Two Final Stories; One Last Lesson

A woman buys a parrot, takes it home, and asks: "Polly want a cracker?"

The parrot responds with a string of vulgar language and epithets.

The woman grabs the parrot and says, "Don't ever use those words in my presence again," and puts it in the freezer.

After an hour or so, she pulls the parrot out and asks if it has learned its lesson and will be good. The parrot replies that he certainly has and will never use foul words again.

Then he adds, "But I do have a question: What did the chicken do?"

Smart parrot!

One look at the frozen chicken and, bingo, he sees the merit in a behavioral change.

The story calls back a childhood memory. I hated spinach. Which meant my mother seemed to serve it at least every other meal. One time I simply refused to eat any. "No," I yelled. "This stuff tastes horrible. It can't be good for me."

I was totally unprepared for my mother's response: "If you don't eat your spinach, you'll grow up to be like Loopy."

That was a powerful retort. No kid wanted to be like crazy Loopy. He walked the neighborhood daily, animatedly talking to himself, trees, birds, cats, dogs and worms, but never (to my knowledge) other humans.

Her admonition had its effect for probably a month or so until I figured out that there was no way I was going to be like Loopy since

(a) I talked to people all the time and (b) I didn't talk to trees, birds and worms. (It was okay, I decided, to talk to cats and dogs since everybody else I knew did it too.)

What's the point of all this?

Well, some lessons take and some don't. It's unlikely the parrot ever forgot the frozen chicken he viewed in the freezer. My mother's lesson had considerably less impact. Loopy went the way of Popeye, with regard to spinach. Neither example of manhood persuaded me that the green, stringy stuff would cause me to be like them.

But the parrot story and the memory of my mother's admonition about spinach got me to thinking about the all the lessons we've learned throughout life. And that provoked me to think about all the lessons I've included in this book.

Looking back, I hope you've learned some significant lessons about life that you'll pass along to others—like your children and grandchildren.

I also hope you've learned some significant lessons about leadership that will help you be a better person and a better leader. Maybe, you've even learned a few that will help you become a servant leader.

If so, that would make me very, very happy!

I wish you well.

Recommended Reading

Behavior

Beer, Stafford, *Platform for Change*, John Wiley, 1975

Buber, Martin, *I and Thou*, Scribner's and Sons, 1958

Damon, William, *Greater Expectations*, The Free Press, 1995

Dohrenwend, Barbara Snell and Bruce P., eds., *Stressful Life Events: Their Nature and Effects*, John Wiley, 1974

Erickson, Erik, H., *Identity: Youth and Crisis*, Norton, 1968

Frankl, Victor, *Man's Search for Meaning*, Washington Square Press, 1963

Fromm, Erich, *To Have or To Be*, Harper & Row, 1976

Gaylin, Willard, *Feelings*, Harper & Row, 1965

Glasser, William, *Take Effective Control of Your Life*, Harper & Row, 1984

Goleman, Daniel, *Emotional Intelligence,* Bantam Books, 1995

Hammerschlag, Carl, *The Theft of the Spirit*, Simon and Schuster, 1978

Keen, Sam, *Fire in the Belly*, Bantam Books, 1991

Klausner, Samuel, ed., *Why Men Take Chances*, Anchor Books, 1968

Layden, Milton, *Escaping the Hostility Trap*, Prentice-Hall, 1977

LeShan, Lawrence, *Alternative Realities*, Evans, 1976

Levinson, Harry, *Emotional Health in the World of Work*, Harper & Row, 1964

Lockland, George T., *Grow or Die*, Delta, 1973

Mahoney, Michael J., *Self-Change*, Norton, 1979

Maslow, Abraham, *Toward a Psychology of Being*, Van Nostrand, 1961

McQuade, Walter and Ann Aikman, *Stress*, Bantam Books, 1974

Menninger, Karl A., *Man Against Himself*, Harcourt, Brace, 1938

———————, *The Vital Balance*, Viking, 1963

———————, *The Human Mind*, Alfred A. Knopf, 1966

Oldham, John M., and Lois B. Morris, *The New Personality Self-Portrait*, Bantam Books, 1995

Peck, Scott, *The Road Less Traveled*, Simon and Schuster, 1978

Pelletier, Kenneth R., *Mind as Healer, Mind as Slayer*, Delta, 1977

Rogers, Carl, *On Becoming a Person*, Houghton-Mifflin, 1970

Selye, Hans, *The Stress of Life*, McGraw-Hill, 1956

———————, *Stress Without Distress*, NAL, 1975

Tillich, Paul, *The Courage to Be*, Yale University Press, 1952

White, Benjamin V., and Helen White, *The Excitement of Change*, Seabury Press, 1975

Leadership

Bakke, Dennis W., *Joy at Work*, PVG, 2005

Bellah, et al, *Habits of the Heart*, University of California Press, 1985

———————, *The Good Society*, Alfred A. Knopf, 1991

Bennis, Warren G., *The Unconscious Conspiracy: Why Leaders Can't Lead*, Amacom, 1976

———————, *On Becoming a Leader*, Basic Books, 2003

Bloch, Peter, *The Empowered Manager*, Jossey-Bass, 1987

Brown, Judith, *Gandhi, Prisoner of Hope*, Yale University Press, 1989

Chappell, Tom, *The Soul of a Business*, Bantam Books, 1993

DePree, Max, *Leadership is an Art*, Dell, 1989

Galbraith, John Kenneth, *The Culture of Contentment*, Houghton-Mifflin, 1992

Gardner, John, *Excellence*, Harper & Row, 1961

_____, *Self-Renewal*, Harper & Row, 1963

Greenleaf, Robert K., *Servant Leadership*, Paulist Press, 1977

_____, *The Servant as Leader*, The Robert K. Greenleaf Center, 1991

Giuliani, Rudolph W., and Ken Kurson, *Leadership*, Miramax, 2002

Hesse, Herman, *Siddhartha*, New Directions, 1951

Jaworski, Joseph, *Synchronicity: The Inner Path of Leadership*, Berrett and Koehler, 1996

Kotter, John P., *Power and Influence*, The Free Press, 1985

Kouzes, James M., and Barry Z. Posner, *The Leadership Challenge*, Jossey-Bass, 2003

Kriegel, Robert J., and Louis Patter, *If It Ain't Broke, Break It!*, Warner Books, 1991

Leonard, George, *The Transformation*, Delacorte, 1972

McGregor, Douglas, *The Human Side of Enterprise*, McGraw-Hill, 1960

Nair, Keshavan, *A Higher Standard of Leadership: Lessons from the Life of Gandhi*, Berrett-Koehler, 1994

Palmer, Parker J., *Leading from Within*, The Servant Leadership School Press, 1995

Peters, Thomas J., and Waterman, Robert H., *In Search of Excellence*, Harper & Row, 1982

Sims, Bennett J., *Servanthood*, Cowley, 1997

Wheatley, Margaret, J., *Leadership and the New Science*, Berrett-Koehler, 1992

Whyte, William H. *The Organization Man*, Simon and Schuster, 1956

Zander, Rosamund Stone, and Benjamin Zander, *The Art of Possibility*, Penguin Books, 2002

About the Author

 A native of Kansas City, Missouri, Ron Barnes was a 1952 graduate of the The College of William and Mary, where he was an All-American tennis player, elected to Omicron Delta Kappa, National Leadership Fraternity, and received the Algernon Sydney Sullivan Award for service to students and the College. Following service in the U.S. Army, with a tour of duty in Korea, he received graduate degrees, including a doctorate in Counseling and Guidance, from the University of Colorado. He worked as an administrator and professor at several universities and colleges, receiving honors as Professor of the Year at Iowa State University and designation as an Outstanding Educator in America.

In the early 1960s, while active in the civil rights movement, he served as National President of the United Campus Christian Fellowship, and Chairman of the National Council of Churches' Commission on Higher Education of the Negro. During the summer of 1964 he was a Visiting Professor at Tuskegee Institute in Alabama. By the early 1970s Ron was Senior Associate and Director of Seminars at The Menninger Foundation in Topeka, Kansas.

Moving to Arizona in the mid 1970s, he developed and owned three human service companies, consulted with or conducted seminars for over two hundred business, government, health care, and educational organizations, and was identified by *Time* and *U.S. News and World Report* magazines as a psychologist, educator and business consultant. After retiring to Prescott, Arizona in 1985, he served on a number of community boards and committees; developed in 1990 the Prescott Area Leadership program; and, in 1997, was recipient of the Prescott Community Visionary Award.